HEBREWS:

Pilgrim's Progress or Regress?

Jim Townsend

DAVID C. COOK PUBLISHING CO.
ELGIN, ILLINOIS • WESTON ONTARIO

To Dr. Haddon Robinson,
stimulator par excellence.

Hebrews: Pilgrim's Progress or Regress?

David C. Cook Publishing Co. 850 North Grove Avenue Elgin, IL 60120 Printed in U.S.A.

Editor: Gary Wilde
Designer: Dawn Lauck
Cover: Bakstad Photographics

ISBN: 1-55513-846-2
Library of Congress Catalog Number:87-70311

CONTENTS

INTRODUCTION

Welcome to the Bible Mastery Series, designed to aid serious Bible students in group settings. Ideally, every student should have a copy of this study manual. Then the group sessions will be spent focusing largely upon the questions and activities at the back of the book in the DIRECTIONS FOR GROUP LEADERS section, p. 124. **Since all participants should have read the up-front commentary before class, the group's time can be spent primarily upon sharing experiences about how to apply these truths to their lives (rather than in factual and interpretive discussions).**

Each chapter contains many quotes and ideas from the best of past and present evangelical scholarship. In effect, I have provided a mini-library of information from the standard, solid commentators that Bible students turn to for interpretation and explanation. In most cases, the Notes section at the back of the book will give sources for the information. I did the digging, you get the results!

The Symbols

Various boxes are set off from the rest of the text. These will give background information or illustrations from such areas as theology, archaeology, original languages, etc. Here is a key to the symbols:

GREEKSPEAK: Concise explanations of important Greek words, tenses, syntax, to help with interpreting the text's meaning.

THEOLOGITALK: Discusses theological terms and doctrinal issues in relation to the text.

CAN YOU DIG IT? Gives valuable cultural insight from archaeology.

QUOTABLE QUOTES: Memorable statements from various sources.

WINDOW ON THE WORD: Anecdotal material to illustrate a point in the text.

THOUGHT QUESTION: A chance to pause and reflect on issues raised in the text.

Outline of Hebrews

All aboard our imaginary airplane, because before jumping right into the verses of Hebrews you will want to soar above it to get a panoramic sweep of the entire book! In a nutshell, Hebrews teaches that "God Has a Better Idea" because of:

I. *The Person Involved (1:1—3:6)—God's Son is superior to:*
   - A. Prophets 1:1-3
   - B. Angels 1:4—2:18
   - C. Moses 3:1-6

The New Covenant is better because of:

II. *The Purpose Intended (3:7—4:13)—to provide redemption rest:*
   - A. Rest is for "today" (3:7, 13, 15; 4:7)
   - B. A rest remains to enter (3:11, 18, 19; 4:1, 3, 5, 6, 9-11)
   - C. Rest is entered by faith (3:12, 18, 19; 4:2, 3, 6)

The New Covenant is better because of:

III. *The Priesthood Interposed (4:14—8:5)*
   - A. Thesis: Jesus is a Priest with credentials like Aaron (4:14—5:10).
   - B. Parenthesis: Before discussing Melchizedek you need maturity—not apostasy (5:11—6:20)!
   - C. Thesis: Jesus is a Priest with a calling like Melchizedek (7:1—8:5).

The New Covenant is better because of:

IV. *The Program Inaugurated (8:6—10:18)*
   - A. The Better Covenant (8:6-13)
   - B. The Better Sanctuary and Service (9:1-10)
   - C. The Better Sacrifice (9:11—10:18)

The New Covenant is better because of:

V. *The Principles and Practices Inspired (10:19—13:25)*
   - A. The peril of faithlessness signaled (10:19-31)
   - B. The principle of faith illustrated (10:38—12:4)
   - C. The process of faith's discipline (12:5-17)
   - D. The peril of faithlessness signaled for the last time (12:18-29)
   - E. The practices of the faith life (13:1-25)

CHAPTER

1

PILGRIM'S PROGRESS OR REGRESS?

Hebrews 1:1-3

One radio spokesperson called stress "the modern saber-toothed tiger." No longer do we venture forth with clubs to face saber-toothed tigers. But stress, just as vicious, can leave us depressed, anxiety ridden, frazzled, or traumatized.

Batsell B. Baxter has a book of sermons entitled *When Life Tumbles In.* If you have ever experienced that "tumbling" feeling (for example, upon learning that your best friend has been diagnosed as having cancer), then probably some past submerged scene comes looming up into your present consciousness.

? Mentally recite a recent experience of deep distress, or some occasion when life seemed to tumble in upon you.

If you can recall being jilted or divorced, told you have a tumor, or told that your child has suddenly been taken to the hospital, then you are ready to enter through the portals of the psyche of the first readers of Hebrews. They, too, felt like everything was coming unglued, that they were living through an emotional earthquake (see vss. 12:27, 28).

By reading Hebrews 10:32-34 and 13:3a, we learn that some of the readers had been pommelled by religious persecution, but none of them had been martyred for their Christianity ("not yet resisted to the point of shedding your blood," 12:4).

If we insert ourselves into their sandals, it is easy to see how they might think,"Why can't we have the best of both worlds? If we just go back to our old Judaism (offer sacrifices, etc.), then maybe the persecution will stop. Why not?"

"Why not go back?" The author's answer is the document we call Hebrews. Would the readers "shrink back" (10:39), or "go on to maturity" (6:1)? Over against the dangers of a *Pilgrim's Regress* (a book title from C. S. Lewis), the author of Hebrews urges his readers to *Pilgrim's Progress.* Don't go back. Go on with Christ! That's the heart of the Book of Hebrews.

BACKGROUND TO THE BOOK

The Purpose of Writing

Why was Hebrews written? E. F. Scott said, "The Epistle to the Hebrews is in many respects the riddle of the New Testament." However, the author's aim in writing does not seem to be as much a riddle as some other features of the book. Here are some of the aims of the author:

1. To send up warning signals, like red flares.
2. To stimulate the readers to go forward spiritually rather than backward.
3. To show the superiority of God's Son over anything and anyone else.

The author is a warner. Hebrews is latticed with a series of five warning passages: 2:1-4; 3:7—4:13; 5:11—6:20; 10:26-39; and 12:15-29. The readers must "not drift away" (2:2); must not turn "away from the living God" (3:12), but must "hold firmly till the end" (3:14); must "go on to maturity" (6:1) rather than "fall away" (6:6); must not "deliberately keep on sinning" (10:26) and "shrink back" (10:39); must not "turn away from him who warns us from heaven" (12:25). These are the author's red flares. Such people, who deliberately and defiantly defect from their former faith, are sometimes labeled apostates.

But the author's aim is not merely negative. Positively, he seeks to prod them to progress. This is demonstrated by the "let us" garden planted throughout the Book of Hebrews (see "let us" in 4:1, 14, 16; 6:1; 10:22-25; 12:1, 28; 13:15).

If the writer is to keep his in-the-lurch readers from spiritual malady, he must prescribe for them an antidote greater than the disease. This he does by showing them that God's "better" idea in the New Covenant is vastly superior to anyone or anything they could conceivably name. God's Son is superior to:

1. Prophets (1:1-3);
2. Angels (1:4—2:18);
3. Moses (3:1-6);
4. Old Testament "rest" (3:7—4:13);
5. Old Testament priesthood (4:14—8:5);
6. The Old Covenant (8:6-13);
7. An earthly sanctuary and sacrifices (9:1—10:18);
8. Any problems we may face (10:19—13:25).

Puzzle Pieces Identifying the Readers

Unlike Paul's unquestionable 13 epistles, we have no "unto the church of the . . ." inset in the opening lines of Hebrews. Who are the mystery readers? Like Sherlock Holmes we can apply our detective skills to this spiritual mystery, since certain clues emerge from the material. Reread Hebrews 10:32-34; 12:4 and 13:3a for clues concerning their contrary circumstances. We have also sketched the recipients' tightrope-walk between regress and progress (read Heb. 3:12; 4:1; 6:1-6; 10:29, 39 and 12:25). Furthermore, what would you assume about the readers' racial makeup from passages like Hebrews 13:10-15? What do you conclude about the addressees from the expression "by this time" in 5:12 (in the context of 5:11-14)?

The Period of Writing

Not only is it difficult to pinpoint the precise place to which Hebrews was written, it is also precarious to dogmatize about the exact time of writing. Read Hebrews 5:1; 7:28; 8:3, 4, 13; 9:9, 25; and 10:22. What verb tenses are mainly used in these verses? Many scholars feel that these present tenses are a tip-off that the whole priest-and-sacrificial system was still operative when the author was writing. If so, that would date Hebrews before A.D. 70, the destruction of Jerusalem and the Jewish Temple—when the sacrificial system ceased. If this is so, the readers could have lived in Palestine.

If the phrase "from Italy" in 13:24 means that some former Italian believers join the author in fondly greeting the readers back home, then Rome might have been the target audience of Hebrews. If this is true, Hebrews 12:4 indicates that no martyrdoms had occurred, demanding a date prior to Nero's death-dealing persecution in Rome,

A.D. 64. The safest time slot for Hebrews seems to be the zone between A.D. 60 and 70, although some scholars place it later.

Possibilities for Authorship

In the King James Version (KJV), the heading over Hebrews is "The Epistle of Paul the Apostle to the Hebrews." But such a heading was not part of the original inspired text. Because there are many reasons for holding that Paul was *not* the author, the majority of orthodox Bible scholars make other suggestions:

Suggested Author	Who Suggested	Pro	Con
Paul	Early tradition popularized by KJV	Author knows Timothy (13:23)	Hebrews does not start like any of Paul's letters.
Barnabas	Tertullian about A.D.200	He was a Levite and "Son of Encouragement" who may have written words of encouragement (Heb. 13:22). The Greek word is the same.	We have no writing samples of Barnabas. He ceases from Acts right before Timothy (chap. 16) enters (Heb. 13:23).
Luke	Clement of Alexandria (A.D.260), and John Calvin.	This would explain the more polished Greek than Paul writes.	Hebrews doesn't focus on subjects similar to Luke's Gospel, or Acts.
Apollos	Martin Luther (A.D. 1500s)	Apollos fits well with the description of Acts 18:24-28.	We have no other samples of Apollos's writing.
Priscilla	Adolph vonHarnack (A.D. 1800s)	A female author might explain the absence of an author's name in that culture.	The masculine gender of the participle in Heb.11:32 argues against a woman author.

Of all the selections in this smorgasbord, I think Apollos best matches the credentials of Hebrews' author. Apollos was a Jewish "native of Alexandria," Egypt (Acts 18:24). Greek scholars can tell that the author of Hebrews regularly quotes from the Greek Old Testament Bible that originated in Alexandria between 250 and 150 B.C. (This Greek Old Testament is called the *Septuagint [Sep-TWO-uh-jihnt].*) Apollos was proficient in the Old Testament (Acts 18:24b). Hebrews is like a graduate course in the Old Testament.

? In Hebrews 2:3, who is the "him"? Who are "those who heard him"? Who must be included in the group called "us"? What do you observe about the "us" and "those who heard him" in regard to the authorship of Hebrews?

Hebrews 2:3 is considered a crucial verse in determining the question of the authorship of the book. Evidently the author umbrellas himself under the pronoun "us" along with his readers. In grouping himself with the "us," he seems to separate himself from the original 12 apostles (or "those who heard him," that is, Jesus). Therefore, most scholars conclude that the author of Hebrews was outside of the apostolic group, being himself a hearer of the apostles. Some scholars go further and assume that the writer was a second-generation Christian.

Jesus' comment on the wind is appropriate to the source of the Book of Hebrews: "You cannot tell where it comes from or where it is going" (Jn. 3:8). Franz Delitzsch said Hebrews was much like one of its chief characters, the mysterious Melchizedek (Heb. 7:3)—we know very little about his origin. The early church leader Origen provided the classic quote on Hebrews' authorship: "Who wrote the book, God alone knows the truth of the matter."

The Nature of the Book

Both in substance and style the Book of Hebrews is like the old tub-shaped Nash Rambler—recognizably unique. First of all, what is it? Hebrews 13:22 provides a two-fold description: (1) a "word of exhortation," and (2) "a short letter." However, there is no "A to B, grace and peace" formula in its first few verses to earmark it as an epistle of the Pauline variety. A. T. Robertson stated, "It begins like a treatise, proceeds like a sermon, and concludes like a letter."[1]

By reading Acts 13:15 and its following context we learn that a "word of exhortation" is a homily or sermon, such as Paul preached in the synagogue at Pisidian Antioch. Hebrews is certainly sermonic in substance. Perhaps, then, we may coin a word to capture the hybrid nature of Hebrews, and call it a "homiletter."

Scholars always comment on the literary beauty of Hebrews.

Classical Greek scholar E. M. Blaiklock said that the author of Hebrews "is a master of style, and coins more quotable phrases per chapter than any other New Testament writer."[2] There are over 160 Greek words that appear only in Hebrews in the New Testament. Probably the stockpile of unusual vocabulary words is due largely to the unique subject matter.

A LOOK AT HEBREWS 1:1-3

A car commercial appeared some years back, claiming "Ford has a better idea." The Book of Hebrews, in capsule form, is one grand message: *God has a better idea.* The better idea is that the New Covenant (or new arrangement) is superior to the Old Covenant. In Hebrews 1:1—3:6 God's idea is better because of the Person involved, namely, God's Son, who is superior to all other persons. Hebrews 1:1—3:6 can be outlined:

God's Son is superior to:

1. The agents of God's message, the prophets (1:1-3);
2. The angels of God who *brought* the old revelation (1:4—2:18);
3. The authority of Moses, who *gave* the old revelation (3:1-6).

God's Final Say-So

Can you recall an experience that seemed like the silence was screaming at you?

"Silence is golden"—unless it lasts for very long. Imagine yourself as the Man in the Iron Mask, stowed away in a dungeon for years with no one to talk to. Silence would probably become deafening.

What if we lived on a silent planet with no communication from God? Plato said, "We must lay hold of the best human opinion in order that carried by it as on a raft we may sail over the dangerous sea of life, unless we can find a stronger boat, or some sure word of God, which will more surely and safely carry us."[3] Must we settle for the flimsy raft of our reasoning, or has God spoken?

"God . . . has spoken" is the lead-off declaration of Hebrews 1:1, 2. In Jeremiah 37:17 the king asked, "Is there any word from the Lord?" The prophet answered, "There is." Those two words contain a titanic truth: "There is" . . . "a more sure word" of God (II Pet. 1:19). We are not left like some lost astronaut whirling aimlessly through empty space. We don't need to devour the horoscopes for some clue from the stars. We don't need to ransack every conceivable philosophy for tips.

We are not left on this planet like a blind illiterate fingering his Braille. God has spoken!

Hebrews 1:1, 2, is a pivotal New Testament passage. In fact, distilled into a single sentence is the whole Bible's fundamental claim! The first sentence, stretching four verses long in the KJV, is like a moss-laden log. We must remove the mossy adverbial modifiers and phrases to uncover how God has spoken.

GOD HAS SPOKEN

	Old Arrangement	*New Arrangement*
How?	in fragmentary fashion	fully and finally
When?	"in the past"	"in these last days"
To Whom?	"to our forefathers"	"to us"
By Whom?	"through the prophets"	"by his Son"

Across from Snowden Junior High School in Memphis, Tennessee, there used to be an almost story-book-like shopping spot that seemed to be a transplant out of the 1940s. In a row of shops stood Burkle's Bakery, an old fashioned drug store with its ice cream counter, and a "sundry" store. The "sundry" store was full of fascinating knicknacks. The KJV of Hebrews 1:1 indicates that God revealed Himself at "sundry times."

Ω The Greek text of Hebrews 1 begins with *polymeros* and *polytropos.* You can see that the words start the same (that's alliteration), sound the same (that's assonance), and end the same (that's rhyme). More literally, they might be translated, "in many parts and in many ways." Both words begin as the words "polytheism," "polysyllabic," or "polysaturated" do in English. We might try to reproduce the stylistic sounds by the coined words "pluripartite" and "multimodal." This means that God didn't say everything He had to say all in one chunk. His communication was more like car parts coming off an assembly line: first the rearview mirror, then the carburetor, then the front seat cushion! The pieces of God's progressive revelation proceeded forward, but God didn't get stuck in a rut.

God values variation (e.g. Job 33:15; Hos. 12:10). God has used many methods to communicate. God is obviously not stuck on doing the same old thing in the same old way. If *He* isn't, why should *we* be? Do we value mime, skits, poetry, drawings, movies, object lessons, costume drama, etc., for communicating God's truth? God is the great Multimedia User. He is the master Surpriser.

We must always keep our receiver mechanisms attuned to whatever frequency God may be using to transmit His message to us. As Pastor John Holland said when the English pilgrims left Holland for the new world, "God shall cause more light to break forth out of His Word." However, John Stott viewed God's communication from another angle when he stated, "The word of God does not come to men today. It has come once and for all. Men must now come to it."[4] In His Son, God has essentially said all He needs to say. Now it's up to us.

Hebrews 1:2-4 might be diagrammed with matching parts as follows:

A. "Appointed heir of all things"
(future heir of creation)
- B. "Through whom He made the universe"
(creating our temporal world)
  - C. "The radiance of God's glory"
(He radiates God's expression)
  - C. "The exact representation of his being"
(He represents God's essence)
- B. "Sustaining all things"
(controlling our spatial world)
  - D. "He . . . provided purification"
(His work was accomplished on earth)
  - D. "He . . . sat down at the right hand" of God
(His work was approved in Heaven)

A. "He has inherited . . . a superior name"
(past heir of a name).

How does knowing that God's Son is "heir of all things" provide you with psychological security?

Seven Scintillating Statements About God's Son

1. God's Son is history's heir. Michael Green said that history "is . . . like a game of chess after the critical move has been played. The game goes on, but it can only have one end."[5] Surely, knowing this provides the mental mountain climber with a firm rope knot for moving onward.

2. Not only does history's ending wind up with God's Son, but history's beginning unwinds from Him (vs. 2), for He made (literally) "the ages." David McCarthy observed, "When Lincoln died, Edwin Stanton, the secretary of war, said, 'Now he belongs to the ages.'

There is only one . . . concerning . . . whom . . . one must turn the sentence around and say, 'The ages belong to Him.' "[6] John 1:3; I Corinthians 8:6; and Colossians 1:16 also affirm Christ's creative role.

While the first two statements concern God's Son in relation to the ending and beginning of our planet, the second pair of statements focuses on the Son in relation to the Father.

3. God's Son is the outshining of God's glory. He had prayed to the Father, "Glorify me . . . with the glory I had with you before the world began" (Jn. 17:5). That "glow-ry" had flared up momentarily at His Transfiguration "like a million floodlights had just been turned on inside Him."[7] Just as there is no light without brightness and no brightness without light, so the Son radiates the Father's light ("God is light," I Jn. 1:5; God "lives in unapproachable light," I Tim. 6:16; Jesus said: "I am the light of the world," Jn. 8:12).

4. The Son is the exact expression of the essence of God: "the exact representation of his being" (1:3). On the ceiling of the Rospigliosi Palace in Rome is Guido Reni's famous fresco, The Aurora. To look very long at such an overhead painting would give one a stiff neck. However, a large mirror near the floor reflects the glory of and affords "the exact representation of" the ceiling masterpiece. This mirroring is what God the Son does for God the Father.

5. The Son is the powerful Person behind providence. What we call "gravity" scientifically, the Bible calls God's Son, for "in him all things hold together" (Col. 1:16). He is the cosmic cement; He is God's glue. In an ancient myth, Atlas was depicted with the dead weight of the world hoisted on his shoulders. By contrast, God's Son upholds the universe by His dynamic utterance.

? When people watch an emotionally cleansing play, they say they've experienced a "catharsis." Can you recall a time when you felt psychologically or spiritually purged?

6. This same Creator-Controller of our universe has come to grips with the root problem in our universe: the sin question. In an ancient myth, the King of Elis was a man named Augeas. He was famed for his 3,000 oxen, including twelve white bulls. One of Hercules' 12 herculean tasks was to clean out Augeas's stables, that had not been cleansed for years. In mythical fashion Hercules accomplished the feat by rerouting the rivers of Alpheus and Peneus to clean the stables.

In our text, the Greek word for "purged" or "provided purification" (NIV) is *katharismon,* from which we derive the term "catharsis." God's close encounter with this planet came with the highest price tag!

When we are informed that God's Son "provided purification for sins," we are tiptoeing close to the central theme of Hebrews. We are being told, "He did what priests do." The midsection of Hebrews (4:14—8:5) explores this concept.

7. Not only has God's Son accomplished a priestly role, but He has been awarded a royal reward: He "sat down at the right hand of the Majesty in heaven" (1:3). When James and John were maneuvering for the position on Jesus' "right hand" (Mk. 10:37), they were vying for the inside track to His highest honor.

August van Ryn explained, "When we say that Queen Elizabeth is on the throne of England, we do not mean that she is always sitting on a throne (I don't believe she ever is), but we mean that she is the reigning monarch."[8] In a sense, the right hand of God is everywhere. Thus, John Calvin, the Reformer, concluded, "To sit at God's right hand is to be helmsman of the universe."[9]

Each clause in these first three verses of Hebrews is a boxcar loaded with highly valuable cargo. Consequently we have seen:

GOD'S SON IS SUPERIOR TO PROPHETS

I. *By comparison with past revelation (1:1)*
   A. Theirs was fragmentary
   B. Theirs was to the forefathers

II. *By the completedness of the last revelation (1:2,3)*
   A. His is full and final
   B. He is featured (in seven statements)
      1. In His work with the world as:
         a. Cosmic heir of all things
         b. Creation's maker of all things
      2. In His relationship to God as:
         a. Effulgence of God's excellencies
         b. Exact expression of God's essence
      3. In His awesome operation of:
         a. Sustaining power of the universe
         b. Sin purification on the cross
         c. Seated posture with the Father

This is Jesus the incomparable!

CHAPTER

2

Above Angels

Hebrews 1:4—2:4

The German writer Goethe said, "Let me name for you an appendage: what you call angels."[1] Goethe's reaction to angels would coincide with that of many modern thinkers, including some theologians. Aren't angels just an appendage, like some luxury chrome or gadget you might or might not choose to purchase with your new car?

Bernard Ramm went on to capture the prevailing modern sentiment: "In the universe of electrons and positrons, atomic energy and rocket power, Einsteinian astronomy and nuclear physics, angels seem out of place. They seem to intrude upon the scene like the unexpected visit of the country relatives to their rich city kinfolk. Atoms seem at home in our contemporary thinking, but not angels!"

No matter what certain modern people may think about angels, the readers of Hebrews were concerned—probably overconcerned—with the subject of angels. One scholar has even argued that the Book of Hebrews was written to Colosse, where some had gotten obsessed with the "worship of angels" (Col. 2:18). Perhaps the receivers of Hebrews were borderline angelolaters. Otherwise, why would the author of Hebrews spend two chapters emphasizing the fact that God's Son is superior to angels?

The Ball Bearing of the Author's Argument

Before we begin an intensive analysis of Hebrews 1:4—2:4, we need an overarching synthesis of the logic of the first two chapters. The thought flow may be traced as follows:

A. The Son's superiority to the angels is shown by a series of seven Scripture quotations (1:5-14);

B. If the message spoken by angels was taken so seriously, how much more seriously ought the message spoken in and by God's Son to be taken (2:1-4);

C. The "world to come" has not been subjected to angels as administrative supervisors, but (implied) to God's glorified Son (2:5-9);

D. The Son assumed human nature (becoming lower than angels) in order to lift redeemed human nature above the angels (2:10-18).

The scene at Sinai (Ex. 19—20) is silent about angels. However, later references to the Law-giving at Sinai include:

1. "The Lord came from Sinai . . . He came with myriads of holy ones" (Deut. 33:2).
2. "The chariots of God are tens of thousands and thousands of thousands; The Lord has come from Sinai" (Ps. 68:17).
3. (Moses) "was . . . with the angel who spoke to him on Mount Sinai; and he received living words to pass on to us" (Acts 7:38).
4. "You have received the law that was put into effect through angels" (Acts 7:53).
5. "The law was put in effect through angels by a mediator" (Gal. 3:19).

From this recital it is easy to see that angelic agents had a role in the giving of the Old Testament Law. Thus, the inner logic of Hebrews 1:4—2:4 runs: The Law was communicated through angels—and that was taken seriously; but the New Testament revelation was communicated through God's Son; therefore, how much more seriously we ought to take *that.*

Seven Scriptural Statements Showing the Son's Superiority to Angels

Just as the author of Hebrews painted a portrait of God's Son in seven picturesque phrases (1:2, 3), so now he uses seven Old Testament quotes to buttress his case that the Son of God is above all angels. By virtue of His Ascension and present session (see the last phrase in vs. 3) the Son "became as much superior to the angels as the name he has inherited is superior to theirs" (1:4). Though He was Son already (Heb. 5:8), yet He "was openly designated as the Son of God with power when He was raised from the dead" (Rom. 1:4, *Berkeley Version.* Compare Eph. 1:19-22 and Phil. 2:9-11.) Therefore, having been raised up from the earth and raised up to Heaven, God's Son could be broadcasted as being so much "better" than the angels. (This Greek word for "better" is found 13 times in Hebrews, and only 6 other times in the New Testament.)

W. F. Albright called the Dead Sea Scrolls "the greatest single manuscript discovery of modern times." The people of the isolated Dead Sea community at Qumran were the equivalent of Jewish monks. The documents of this community reveal that they expected two (!) messiahs—a royal, or Davidic Messiah and a priestly, or Aaronic Messiah. Furthermore, there is evidence that they considered both of these Messiahs to be subordinate to the archangel Michael. This is exactly the sort of view the author of Hebrews appears to be counteracting in Hebrews 1 and 2.

Hillel was a great Jewish rabbi who formulated some rules for interpretation, one of which was called the "light and heavy." It was as if one were to weigh two ideas on a scale to see which turned out to be the heavier or more important. In Hebrews 1 our author seems to be using this "light and heavy" formula, by weighing the angels against God's Son.

Like an army sergeant, he issues orders for seven Old Testament passages to fall into ranks in support of the Son of God! The writer selected five out of the seven passages from Psalms. In fact, about one-third of all the author's quotations are culled from the Psalms.

1. Psalm 2:7 is his first quote. In Psalm 2 we find:
   (a) the Lord (2:2);
   (b) the Lord's "Anointed," or Messiah (2:2), who is installed as King on Mount Zion in Jerusalem (2:6).

In the psalm the Lord says to the King/Messiah:

> "You are my Son;
> Today I have become your Father" (2:7).

Many scholars think that in this psalm's immediate context the Hebrew king is being adopted as God's "son" at his installment ceremony. However, the New Testament frequently applies this text to God's Messianic Son (see Mk. 1:11), particularly to the day of His resurrection (see Acts 13:33, 34). The angels were apparently called collectively "sons of God" in the plural in the Old Testament (see Job 1:6; 38:7). However, never does God single out one angel to label him a Son.

2. To further document this point, the author resorts to II Sam. 7:14. Verses 12-16 of this chapter are commonly called the Davidic Covenant. Obviously, in its short-range context, II Sam. 7:14 is talking about David's descendants ("when he does wrong").

Nevertheless, in its long-range fulfillment it comes to focus in David's greatest Son (Lk. 1:32, 33). David's house, kingdom, and throne were not established "forever" in Solomon, David's immediate heir. In the covenant an eternal Father-Son relationship is validated.

3. In Hebrews 1:6 the author quotes Deuteronomy 32:43 from the Greek version of the Old Testament. The interesting thing about the Old Testament quotation in Hebrews 1:6 is that the text quoted is not found in our present standard text of the Hebrew Old Testament at all. But it *is* found in the Septuagint. However, when the Dead Sea Scrolls were discovered, a Hebrew copy was found that did contain these words from Deuteronomy 32: 43.

? Note the difference between the KJV ("And again, when he bringeth in the first begotten into the world") and the New King James Version ("And when He again brings the firstborn into the world") in terms of the position of the word "again." What would be the difference in the meaning of each translation?

In the case of the KJV the "again" would simply indicate another Old Testament verse is being added to the lineup of prooftexts. If the NKJV is selected, the writer of Hebrews is talking about Christ's Second Coming. (These two closely related translations show us at this point that translators differ in how they may interpret any given word.)

Whether this angel worship of God's Son in Hebrews 1:6 refers to His first coming (Lk. 2:9-14) or His Second Coming (Mt. 24:29-31), in either case it is the Son who is being worshiped. Angels are not to be worshiped (see Col. 2:18, and Rev. 19:10 in its preceding context). This means that the Son is truly God (Jn. 1:1; 5:18; 10:33; 20:28; Rev. 19:10).

4. Hebrews 1:7 quotes Psalm 104:4. This is a nature psalm. In it angels are compared to wind (the margin rendering of "spirits" in the KJV), and lightning flashes function as God's servants. Henry Longfellow did an imaginative takeoff on this idea:

> The Angels of Wind and of Fire
> Chant only one hymn and expire
> With the song's irresistable stress;
> Expire in their rapture and wonder,
> As harp-strings are broken asunder
> By music they throb to express!

In the supersaunalike heat of God's presence the angels' harp strings are popping and they "chant only one hymn and expire." This imaginative idea of Longfellow's found a similar portrayal in the "schmoos" of the Little Abner comic strip some years ago. Schmoos were lovable, round, little ghostlike creatures who would perform some task for you; then "poof"—they went out of existence.

Jim Elliot, martyred by Auca Indians in South America, wrote on this text: "He makes his ministers 'a flame of fire'; am I ignitible? God deliver me from the dread asbestos of 'other things!' "

What do you think Jim Elliot meant by being "ignitible for God"? Name some "other things" that can act as asbestos in our lives to keep us from burning brightly for God.

5. Hebrews 1:8 quotes Psalm 45:6, 7. This psalm is a wedding song for one of Israel's kings. Just as Old Testament judges had been addressed as "gods" (for acting in a God role) in Psalm 32:6 (quoted in Jn. 10:34), so also an Old Testament king may have been addressed as "God" in Psalm 45:6. To circumvent this seeming problem, numerous translators adopted the translation, "God is your throne for ever and ever" (so Wycliffe, Tyndale, Westcott, Moffatt, and the margins of the RSV and NEB). However, that translation would make little sense if carried over into Hebrews 1:8. Hence, the traditional translation is adopted by the NIV, Williams, Berkeley, J. B. Phillips, and The Good News Bible. The Son is directly addressed here as "God."

Once Queen Esther had risked her life with King Xerxes of Persia by approaching his throne without permission. To her Xerxes graciously "held out . . . the gold scepter" (Esth. 5:2). For her, it was a scepter of acceptance. God's Son rules with a scepter of righteousness (Heb. 1:8).

Is it wrong to hate?

Hating sin is not sin (Heb. 1:9). The poet Robert Browning wrote:

> Like Dante, he loved well, because he hated;
> Hated wickedness, and all that hinders loving.

Charles Wesley penned:

> Thou hatest all iniquity
> But nothing Thou hast made.
> Oh may I learn Thy art,
> With meekness to reprove;
> To hate the sin with all my heart,
> But still the sinner love.

Maybe we had better learn to be better haters! John Wesley proclaimed, "Give me a hundred men who fear nothing but God, and who *hate* nothing but sin, and who know nothing but Jesus Christ and Him crucified, and I will shake the world."

C. S. Lewis, scholarly British champion of Christianity, questioned whether we could "hate the sin, but love the sinner" until one day he realized that that is the way we rather consistently act toward ourselves if we are psychologically normal people. We do not write ourselves off even for some repeated sin, but rather love ourselves (Mt. 22:39). Therefore, why not treat others as we treat ourselves?

Can you give a real-life recent illustration of someone hating *properly*?

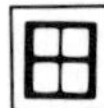

Norma and Wilbur Craig were walking one evening in a local park when they encountered a small boy tied up to a parking lot rail. Three women stood by laughing at him. The Craigs asked, "What's going on here?" They were told to mind their own business and that one of the women was the child's mother. "Haven't you heard of child abuse?" they countered. With that they were cussed out. They sought police who ordinarily cruised the park but none were to be found.

Radio talk-show psychologist, Dr. Toni Grant, received a call from a female listener who wanted to know why her husband's male friends all seemed to get the wrong idea from her friendliness in group gatherings. The woman said that the men called her up later when her husband wasn't home. This woman, who didn't regard herself as pretty, would tell them her husband wasn't home—and they would reply that that's why they were calling. Dr. Grant pointed out that at no point in the conversation did the woman ever raise her voice. She spoke in a soft and sultry voice. In order to deal decisively with the callers, Dr. Grant informed her that she would have to tell these men in no uncertain terms not to phone her and she would have to change her honeyed voice with them during social settings. She would have to get mad when she *ought* to be getting mad.

6. The most extensive quote so far, nestled in Hebrews 1:10-12, is derived from Psalm 102:25-27. The poetry of Psalm 102 depicts the world as God's wardrobe. Just as we have fall fashions, winter wear, and spring attire, so God is portrayed (in Heb. 1:11) as clothed in Creation. Creation boasts God's designer label. William Barclay observed that Sir Christopher Wren lies buried in St. Paul's Cathedral, the church he had planned and constructed. There is a Latin inscription on Wren's tombstone that (when translated) reads: "If you wish to see his monument, look around you." In the same way, God's global garments are His monument.

Creation changes. Like moth-eaten clothing it is discarded. Christ the Creator "remains the same" (Heb. 1:12). This unchangingness is called by theologians His immutability (see Mal. 3:6 and Heb. 13:8).

> My love is often low,
> My joy still ebbs and flows;
> But peace with Him remains the same;
> No change Jehovah knows.
> I change, He changes not;
> The Christ can never die:
> His love, not mine, the resting place,
> His truth, not mine, the tie.
> —Horatius Bonar

7. Psalm 110:1 is quoted in Hebrews 1:13. Psalm 110 is one of the principal sermon texts of the New Testament (as we will see in Heb. 5—7). Note that the author of Hebrews concludes just as he commenced his seven citations (1:13—"To which of the angels did God ever say"; see 1:5 for the kickoff text).

The author asks if God ever asked an angel to sit anywhere (1:13; contrast 1:3). Reviewing the Scriptures, we see that angels are never asked to be seated. God never honored an angel as He did His Son.

Hebrews 1:14 has some overtones of Psalm 103:20, 21. Jay Kesler, president of Taylor University, told of staying in a faraway Eastern land. To protect him, his hosts had supplied Kesler with a native who stood outside his window as Kesler lay in a mosquito-netted bed. Kesler said he could hardly sleep that night because of the presence of his watcher. Westerners are not used to such ever-present watchers. One is reminded of John Milton's lines about angels:

> Thousands at his bidding speed
> And post o'er land and ocean without rest;
> They also serve who only stand and wait.

Thus angels are described in Heb. 1:14 as servant-waiters, serving "those who will inherit salvation." Just as Chester Proudfoot assisted Marshall Dillon in *Gunsmoke,* so angels in some way assist believers.

The Danger of Drifting

Hebrews 2:1-4 is the hinge upon which the author's argument to this point swivels. It is the first of five major warning passages in Hebrews. In fact, over half of all Hebrews's verses admonish the readers to continue in steadfast faith.

If God's message via angels (the old arrangement) was taken seriously (2:2), how much more seriously (2:1) must the message conveyed by God's Son (the new arrangement) be taken.

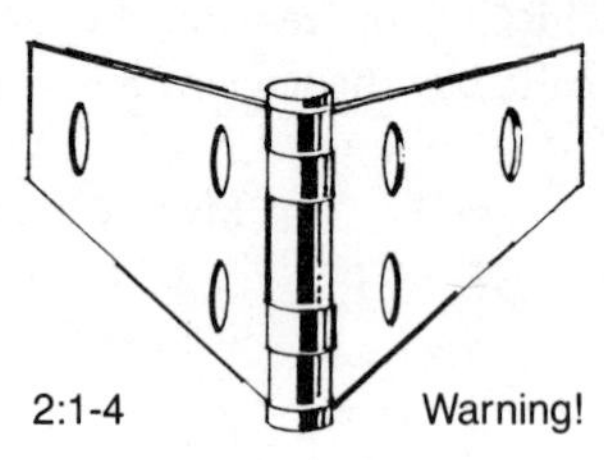

Those skilled in the preacher's craft would call this "verdictive" preaching. This preacher is not merely insinuating to his congregation, "It was nice to have you with us today." His preaching packs a wallop.

As the preacher navigates his way through his sermon, he drops a number of navigational terms. The verb in 2:1 ("we must pay more careful attention") literally means "to hold to"; that is, "to hold [the mind] to." William Barclay says it "can mean to moor a ship."[2] For moorings we must anchor our ship-of-soul at the dock of salvation.

F. B. Meyer wrote:

> *"Consider God's scheme of salvation as a great harbor. After a wild night we have gone down to the harbor, over whose arms the angry waves have been dashing with boom of thunder and in clouds of spray. Outside, the sea has been tossing and churning; the cloudrack driving hurriedly across the sky; the wind howling like the furies of the old fables. But within those glorious walls, the barks which had put in during the night were riding in safety; the sailors resting, or repairing rents in sail and tackle, whilst the waters were unstirred by the storm raging without. Room in it for whole navies of souls to ride at anchor. There is a vessel once manned by seven devils, a pirate ship, but captured by our Emmanuel; and at her stern the name Mary of Magdala. And here one dismasted, and almost shattered . . . and on her stern the words,* The Dying Thief. *And there another . . . now flying a pennon from the masthead,* Chief of Sinners *and* Least of Saints. *And all around a forest of masts . . . ."*[3]

Ω Philip Hughes says that the verb "slip" in 2:1 (KJV) "means literally to 'flow by' or to 'slip away.' Plato uses it of something slipping from one's memory . . . and Plutarch of a ring slipping from a finger . . . and Aristotle of a crumb going down the wrong way . . . ."[4] This verb is found only here in the New Testament. Instead of docking the ship of our soul in the heavenly harbor, we run the danger of drifting.

> One ship drives east, another drives west
> With the self-same winds that blow;
> 'Tis the set of the sails and not the gales
> Which tells us the way to go.

Like the ways of ships are the ways of men
As they sail o'er the sea of life.
It's the set of the soul that determines the goal,
And not the storm and the strife.
—Ella Wheeler Wilcox

F. W. Boreham wrote in a similar vein, but negatively, concerning the English novelist George Eliot (pseudonymn of Mary Ann Evans):

Her anchor relinquished its hold, and almost imperceptibly, she drifted. Principal Fairbairn put it: "She glided out of the faith as easily and as softly as if she had been a ship obeying wind and tide, and her faith a sea that opened silently before and closed noiselessly behind her."[5]

? F. B. Meyer[6] said, "Life's ocean is full of currents, any one of which will sweep us past the harbor mouth . . . and carry us far out to sea . . . until the coastline of heaven recedes." What are some dangerous currents that you have seen carrying people you have known away from the harbor in Christ?

The danger of drifting is so perilous because it is "such a great salvation" (2:3). Comparing our "great salvation" to an ocean, one can always contemplate its ever-expanding horizons.

We only see a little of the ocean,
A few miles distance from the rocky shore;
But, oh, out there beyond the eye's horizon,
There's more!

"The story is related of a poor woman, accustomed to the pinch of poverty in nineteenth-century England, who toiled in a cotton factory in one of the manufacturing towns of Lancashire. On an excursion she went for the first time to the coast. When she got her initial view of the Irish Sea . . . the limitlessness of the ocean with its billows rolling in, she cried out as she drew a long breath of satisfaction: 'At last here comes something there's enough of.' "[7]

? In what ways is salvation great? At what moments have you realized this?

We are urged to dock in the harbor of salvation for three reasons (2:3, 4). This salvation:

1. Was conveyed directly "by the Lord" (that is, Jesus);
2. Was "confirmed to us by those who heard him" (the Lord Jesus);
3. Was corroborated by miracles from the Spirit (2:4).

? How is Christ both the medium and the message?

First, the new arrangement was communicated personally and directly "by the Lord" (2:3). We often think of Jesus as being our message—and He is (I Cor. 1:23; 2:2; II Cor. 1:19; 4:5). But the message is also, in this case, the medium of the message. The word was brought by the Word (Jn. 1:1). Not only is Christ "our peace" (Eph. 2:14), but He "came and preached peace" (Eph. 2:17). God's Son is both the object and subject of the Gospel.

Secondly, the message was "confirmed to us by those who heard him" (2:3). "Those who heard him" (that is, the Lord Jesus) must be the apostles. But notice how the author brackets himself ("us") with his readers in a group separable from the apostles.

1. "The Lord" (Jesus);
2. "Those who heard him" (the apostles);
3. "us" (the author and his readers).

The author of Hebrews, then, did not claim to *be* an apostle (ruling out one of the twelve as its author) and he derived his message *from* the apostles (thereby ruling out Paul as Hebrews's author; see Gal. 1:12, 15-19).

Thirdly, the Gospel message was corroborated by miracles. The New Testament employs a stock vocabulary for miracles—with three of the terms appearing in 2:4 ("signs, wonders, and various miracles"—the last Greek word literally meaning "powers").

HIGHLIGHTS OF MIRACLES

	Response	*Description*	*Purpose*
WONDERS	"Wow!"	portents	attract an audience by awesomeness
POWERS	"Whammo!"	powerful	display divine dynamic
SIGNS	"Why?"	purposeful	have supernatural significance

The same trio of terms appears at Acts 2:22 and II Cor. 12:12. The duo of "signs and wonders" are coupled together twelve times in the New Testament, nine of them being found in Acts. These miracles:

1. Validated the apostles' message.
2. Were "distributed according to His will" (2:4)

These signs share *sign*-ificance. They are pointers beyond themselves. A modern traveler would not think of stopping and unpacking the suitcases from his car trunk upon arrival at a large, green, rectangular U.S. highway sign. Neither should one become obsessed with miracles. Such "signs" function as pointers from "the finger of God" (Lk. 11:20) to a greater destination point, namely, the significance of God's Son.

OUR OUTLINE TO THIS POINT

I. *God's Son is superior to the prophets (1:1-3)*

II. *God's Son is superior to the angels (1:4—2:18)*
   A. As an agent of revelation (1:4—2:4)
   B. As an administrator over Creation (2:5-18)

CHAPTER 3

FRATERNITY OF FLESH

Hebrews 2:5—3:6

Angels: Spiritual Administrators

Modern space fantasies have been filled with vulcans, wookies, droids, imperial walkers, sandworms, ewoks, klingons, banthas, tontons, and other interplanetary creatures. In over half the Bible books we find creatures called angels.

Some students of Scripture have theorized from the "rulers . . . authorities . . . powers . . . and spiritual forces" of Ephesians 6:12 that there are angelic ranks, such as general, colonel, major, sergeant, etc., in God's army of angels. Certainly the Bible speaks of an archangel.

Also, in the Book of Daniel, we get the impression of angelic beings assigned as national administrators. Michael the archangel is called "your [Israel's] prince" (Dan. 10:21), and there are princes for Persia and Greece (Dan. 10:20) who appear to be celestial creatures. This is a fascinating idea—spiritual supervisors in international affairs.

Yet the takeoff point for Hebrews 2:5 is that "it is not to angels that he [God] has subjected the world to come." This, then, is our author's second reason for talking about angels ("The world to come . . . is our theme," NEB).

1:4—2:4—Angels have been special agents of God's old revelation (but God's Son brought the last revelation).

2:5-18—Angels have been spiritual administrators over nations (but God's Son is over "the world to come").

In Bible study, ordinarily one ought to look for logical linkups between paragraphs and verses. At first glance there does not appear to be any hookup between Hebrews 2:4 and 2:5. That is, what does the distribution of miracles (2:4) have to do with "the world to come" (2:5)? The cementing clue, however, is found in Hebrews 6:5 where the author spoke of "the powers of the world to come" (KJV). "Powers" is the literal translation of miracles. In other words, in the author's mind there was a definite connection between miracles and the coming age. Therefore, when he mentioned various versions of miracles in 2:4, it triggered in his mind the idea of the coming age.

Modern indented versions help us see the poetic pattern at an immediate glance. Psalm 8:4-6 reads:

> What is man that you are mindful of him,
> the son of man that you care for him?
> You made him a little lower than the heavenly beings
> and crowned him with glory and honor.
> You made him ruler over the works of your hands;
> you put everything under his feet.

Usually Hebrew poetry is patterned like railroad ties—two parallel lines running side by side. Note the first two lines charted below with their parallel counterparts:

Man	-	Son of man
that you	-	that you
are mindful of	-	care for
him	-	him

Here is one place where the KJV is more helpful than the NIV. The KJV has "put in subjection" in both 2:5 and 2:8, representing the same Greek word. In other words, from the KJV we can see that the author's theme in 2:5 has triggered a recollection of certain Old Testament language in his head.

? Can you pick out the three expressions from Psalm 8:4-6 that the author of Hebrews hoists out to apply to Jesus?

The human race was crowned as caretaker of Creation in Genesis 2 and 3. But humanity muffed it. Smog clouds, extinct animal species, polluted rivers, and illegal chemical waste dumps shout that humanity has muffed it. Humanity's crown as king of Creation is tilted, to say the least. We see nature "red in tooth and claw," as Thomas Hobbes said. Whatever *is* certainly isn't what *ought to be* between us and our universe. Do we see everything put under the human caretaker? No!

Once I was in a Humanities class in college, listening to a magnificent piece of classical music. During the masterpiece came a sound down the corridor outside the classroom—scrape, scrape, scrape! It was a handicapped student struggling along on his crutches. I will never forget the incongruity of sound. Similarly, as our author looks around, first at nature, then at Scripture, he senses a dreadful disharmony. Something is scraping badly. Our world has something rasping about it. It can give us the same shivery sensation we feel when fingernails are scraped across the chalkboard. Can anything be done to recapture humanity's crown rights over Creation?

? If you were God, how would you straighten out an out-of-kilter planet like ours? (See Rom. 8:21, 22.)

Jesus, Superior Administrator

The implied message of this section of Hebrews is that Christ has condescended to recapture the crown rights to Creation that humanity forfeited in the fall of Genesis 3.

In Hebrews 2, however, because of the poetic parallelism (called *synonymous parallelism* when the two lines of poetry say essentially the same thing) of Psalm 8, "son of man" refers primarily to humanity (cp. Num. 23:19 and Jer. 49:18 in the KJV). Humanity was put over God's Creation and God's Creation was put under this kinglet, say the psalm lines (Heb. 2:7, 8). Therefore, Psalm 8 makes the central point that the author of Hebrews wishes to make—Creation's caretaker was not forecast as being angelic, but human.

Here is our author's dilemma:

Bible: Creation will be under a human.
Author: I don't see creation under a human.
God's solution: Jesus, the ideal human.

In Biblical language the author wrote: "But now we see not yet all things put under him [man]. But we see Jesus [the ideal, representative human] . . ." (2:8b, 9a, KJV). For the first time in the Book of Hebrews the name "Jesus" appears.

In other words, the author of Hebrews visualized Jesus as the human *par-excellence.* Whereas humanity flunked its test, the ideal human (Jesus) passed with flying colors. Whereas the first Adam bombed out, "the Last Adam" (I Cor. 15:45) succeeded masterfully. Where we were deficient, Jesus was more than proficient. Jesus fulfilled the psalmist's great expectations. Indeed, Jesus can fulfill our fondest dreams. In thinking about what Jesus had done for and in her, one hymn writer said: "More wonderful it seems than all the golden fancies of all our golden dreams." B. J. Thomas, a former drug addict, said of Jesus in song: "Storybook reality is what he gave to me, for every day he makes my dreams come true."

? How has Jesus fulfilled some dream of yours?

The author of Hebrews agrees with the cut-and-dried logic from Psalm 8: "In putting everything under him [man], God left nothing that is not subject to him" (2:8). *Every*thing excludes *no*thing, right? Right. That's certainly airtight logic!

How then do we explain the fact that we don't see everything functioning smoothly and blissfully under humanity? The missing link is Jesus. At this point the author of Hebrews extracts two more applicable phrases from Psalm 8: "made . . . a little lower than the angels" and "crowned . . . with glory and honor." Jesus wore a crown of thorns in order to be "crowned with glory and honor." God's Son, who was so "much superior to the angels" (Heb. 1:4) "was made a little lower than the angels" (2:9).

? In what ways is Jesus a paradox because of His deity and humanity?

THE PARADOXICAL JESUS

Crowned with thorns	Crowned with glory
Above angels (1:4)	Below angels (2:9)
Son of God (1:2)	Son of Man (2:6)
"With God" (Jn. 1:1)	"Was God" (Jn. 1:1)
"I and the Father are one" (Jn. 10:30)	"The Father is greater than I" (Jn. 14:28)

No wonder the poet could say:

> The nails that pierced His hands were mined
> In secret places He designed;
> He died upon a cross of wood,
> Yet made the hill on which it stood.

In what way was Jesus "made a little lower than the angels"? In what way was Jesus "crowned with glory and honor"? The answer to both questions lies in that "he suffered death." His condescension was the prelude to suffering, and His elevation was the postlude to suffering (see also Phil. 2:8, 9).

In the old cowboy shows when six-shooters brought down a villain, the expression "he bit the dust" was often used for his death. Similarly, Hebrews 2:9 (KJV) says expressively that Jesus "taste[d] death." This death was "for everyone" (2:9). Vincent Taylor stated that "the vicarious [that is, on behalf of others] deed of Christ . . . is the most fundamental note in the teaching of the Epistle."[1]

Hebrews 2:10 transports us, as it were, inside the pages of the ethical etiquette book of God. The Britisher J. B. Phillips has: "It was right and proper." In Homer's *Iliad*, the bard has Juno, queen of the gods, say to Vulcan (in effect): "Son, it's not the etiquette of the gods to suffer on behalf of humans." How thankful we can be that in God's true etiquette God's Son has fittingly suffered on our behalf!

The title "author of their salvation" (2:10) is variously translated. The Greek word here for "author" is used in other Greek literature to describe the legendary champion Hercules. In a sense, Christ is our Champion. F. F. Bruce declared, "He is the Pathfinder, the Pioneer of our salvation. He is the Savior who blazed the trail of salvation . . . . The word . . . appears four times in the NT, the other three being in . . . [Hebrews] 12:2; Acts 3:15; 5:31."[2]

In Hebrews 2:11-13 the author shows the solidarity of God's Son and the "many sons" (2:10) who follow in His glory train. The Sanctifier (the Son) and the "sanctifiees" (the many sons) share a unity (2:11), as documented by the fact that He calls them by the family term "brothers" (2:11).

The first quote welding together the Son and His sons is Psalm 22:22. Early Christians had quickly pinpointed this as a Messianic Psalm (see Ps. 22:1 in Mt. 27:46). From the same psalm the author of Hebrews lifts Psalm 22:22,

> "I will declare your name to my brothers;
> in the congregation I will praise you."

Hebrews 2:12 has: "I will sing your praises." We do know of one instance where Jesus sang (Mk. 14:26). One hymn writer, F. C. Jennings, on the basis of Psalm 22:22, thought imaginatively of our Lord as the musical Maestro leading the great future celestial choir:

> Hark, my soul! Thy Savior sings;
> Catch the joy that music brings;
> And, with that sweet flood of song,
> Pour thy whispering praise along.

How do you feel, being Jesus' "brother"?

Next, the author split Isaiah 8:17, 18 into two quotes, involving "the children God has given me." God's present to Christ consists of "children."

Confucius, the sage of ancient China, was wed at nineteen. Buddha had a wife and child, though he left both on the day of the baby's birth to begin the religious quest. Mohammed was a father, and permitted each of his male followers a maximum of four wives. Yet Jesus never married. However, significantly, Isa. 53:10 speaks of Messiah's offspring.

—Ian Macpherson, *God's Middleman*

If Hebrews 2:9-13 has shown that the Son shares a solidarity with the "many sons," Hebrews 2:14-16 argues that if the "children" of verses 13 and 14 are human, then Jesus also assumed human nature to share *this* solidarity.

In this section of Hebrews (2:9-18) we encounter the most clearly defined statement in the New Testament concerning the "why?" of the plan of salvation.

Below, fill in the space in the right column, telling in a few words why Christ came, or what He came to do.

Reference **Reasons for Christ's Coming**

Mt. 5:17 ______________________________

____

Mk. 10:45 ______________________________

____

Lk. 4:43 ______________________________

____

Lk. 19:10 ______________________________

____

Jn. 3:17 ______________________________

____

Jn. 4:34 ______________________________

____

Jn. 6:33 ______________________________

____

Jn. 6:38 ______________________________

____

Jn. 10:10 ______________________________

____

Rom. 8:3 ______________________________

____

Heb. 2:14, 15 (2) ______________________________

____

Heb. 2:17 ______________________________

____

I Jn. 3:5 ______________________________

____

In Charles Godfrey Gumpel's *How the Devil Was Caught—A Chess Legend*, the Devil was supposed to have engaged in a chess game. He was told he would be checkmated in 7 moves. On the seventh turn he is supposed to have fled, having been checkmated by chessmen in the pattern of the sign of the cross.[3] Jesus came for a two-pronged purpose: (1) to defeat the Devil, and (2) to deliver the death fearers (Heb. 2:14, 15). Thus, David Hubbard remarked, "We are spectators at death's funeral. In the amphitheater of life the grisly gladiator has been downned." S. W. Gandy enshrined this idea poetically:

He hell in hell laid low,
Made sin, He sin o'erthrew,
Bowed to the grave, destroyed it so,
And death, by dying slew.

" He who pretends to face death without fear is a liar.

—Philosopher Jean Jacques Rousseau

No rational man can die without uneasy apprehension.

—Dr. Samuel Johnson

Carlos Baker of Princeton, biographer for Ernest Hemingway, wrote of his subject: "The small boy who shouted 'fraid o' nothing' became the man who discovered that there was plenty to fear, including that vast cosmic nothingness which Goya [the painter] named *Nada.*"

The Son did not enter the arena of angels to assume their nature (2:16) or to "give help to" (NEB) them. Instead, Jesus is our nature-sharer. Consequently, Jesus could "become a merciful and faithful high priest" (2:17). For the first time the writer of Hebrews explicitly calls Jesus a "high priest." Jesus is "merciful" in regard to humans and "faithful" in regard to God.

Christian theology has a lot of *-tion* terms, words ending in *-tion* (salvation, reconciliation, redemption, justification, sanctification, propitiation, glorification, etc.).

The King James Version of Hebrews 2:18, "to make reconciliation," is not the best translation here. Translations vary between the

RSV: "to make expiation for"
(ex-pee-AY-shun)

and

ASV: "to make propitiation for"
(pro-pish-ee-AY-shun).

What is the difference in these two terms? *Expiation* focuses mainly on a sacrifice for sins, whereas *propitiation* emphasizes more the holy anger of God. Orthodox scholars differ in their views regarding which aspect should be emphasized here. F. F. Bruce and Leon Morris believe *propitiation* is correct, whereas B. F. Westcott and Bruce Metzger hold that *expiation* is in view. The NIV seems to adopt a combined meaning by translating the verb "make atonement for."

Propitiation is set against the backdrop of "the wrath of God" (see Rom. 1:18 and I Thess. 1:10). In holy recoil against sin, God's violated righteousness must have atonement. A person has been offended, and settlement must be made. *Expiation* contains no special notion of appeasing an offended deity.

Moses: Servant/Administrator

The mention of a "faithful high priest" (2:17) prompted another takeoff point for our author ("high priest," [3:1] "faithful," [3:2]). Who else was preeminently faithful? Why, Moses, of course. Furthermore, the author has been discussing (in chaps. 1 and 2) angels who are go-betweens in giving God's message. Angels were *celestial* go-betweens in conveying the message at Sinai (Acts 7:53; Gal. 3:19; Hebrews 2:2). But what about the *human* go-between (Moses) who conveyed God's message at Sinai?

Therefore, the writer of Hebrews now makes his third point of comparison with God's Son. God's Son is greater than:

(1) prophets (1:1-3);
(2) angels (1:4—2:18);
(3) Moses (3:1-6).

All three groups were communicators of God's revelation under the old arrangement. Hence, the author now turns to the greatest figure in Old Testament history: Moses.

In what ways is Jesus your Apostle and Priest?

The two titles show two crucial roles of Jesus. An apostle represents God to humanity; a high priest represents humanity to God. "Apostle" means "sent one." Nowhere else in the New Testament is Jesus ever calledan Apostle (though John's Gospel does treat the apostolic idea: Jn. 5:24, 30; 6:29, 38; 7:29). Furthermore, of all New Testament books, only Hebrews explicitly treats Christ's priesthood at length.

Note the comparisons and contrasts from 3:1-6:

Moses	*God's Son*
Faithful (3:2)	Faithful (3:2)
In the house (3:2, 5)	Over the house (3:6)
	Housebuilder (3:3)
Servant (3:5) (See Jn. 8:35.)	Son (3:6)

Our author draws from two Old Testament passages—Numbers 12:7 and Zechariah 6:12.

The key idea in any servant relationship is faithfulness (see I Cor. 4:2). Both Moses the servant and Jesus the Son are described as faithful in Hebrews 3:1-6.

If "Moses was faithful" (3:2, 5) and "Christ is faithful" (3:6), surely this faithfulness ought to rub off on the followers of Christ. This is implied by the takeoff point in 3:6b, and, in the next section (Heb. 3:7-14), will become a vital point: *be faithful.* Faithfulness, like car care, requires maintenance.

Preview: Having demonstrated the superiority of the Son (over prophets, 1:1-3; over angels, 1:4—2:18; over Moses, 3:1-6), the author will now turn to the readers' response to this superior Son of God (in 3:7—4:13).

CHAPTER

4

BRATS AND BELIEF

Hebrews 3:7—4:13

Tripping hither, tripping thither
    Nobody knows the why or whither.
If you ask the special function
    Of our never ceasing motion,
We reply without compunction
    That we haven't any notion.
                    —*poet unknown*

Restless people often rev up their lives with frenetic activity.

? Recall a period in your life when you felt restless. Do you know what caused it? How was it resolved? Look up Hebrews 3:11, 18, 19; 4:1, 3, 5, 6, and 9. What phrase peppers this passage?

The author of Hebrews is a superlative sermonizer. Throughout this homiletter we find his preaching texts. At this juncture the author quotes Psalm 95:7-11, which closes with the clincher: "They shall never enter my [God's] rest." Hebrews 3:7—4:13 revolves around this recurring theme of God's rest. The author's point, driven home in 4:9, is that there is a rest remaining for you. Will you receive God's rest?

Let's backtrack for a moment to reconstruct where we are in the flow of Hebrews. In popular style we might say: God has a better idea! That's what Hebrews has to say. God's idea is better because of:

I. *The person involved: the superior Son and high priest (1:1—3:6).*

II. *The purpose intended: to provide people with redemptive rest (3:7—4:13).*

Faithfulness Required

In Hebrews 3:5, 6 the author made a comparison. Both Moses and the

Messiah were faithful in their calling. That might trigger in the readers' minds the question: Am I faithful? Do I persist in my faith? In Hebrews 3:7—4:13 this becomes the absorbing, though unspoken, question: *Am I faithful in my faith?*

To appreciate the author's argument, read Exodus 17:1-7 and Numbers 14:20-35 for background. Psalm 95:7b-11 was probably sung by Jews in their Sabbath worship at the Temple, making our author's quote all the more meaningful. (Note in 3:7 that for the author, when Scripture speaks, the Spirit speaks.)

? What key word recurs at least five times in Hebrews 3:7, 13, 15, and 4:7? What lesson do you think God is trying to teach us through this?

F. B. Meyer wrote, "Beware of the ossification [or hardening] of the heart. The chalk which now holds the fossil shells was once moist ooze. The horny hand of toil was once full of soft dimples. The murderer once shuddered, when as a boy, he crushed a worm.

"Hearts harden gradually like the freezing of a pond on a frosty night. At first . . . there is a thin film of ice, so slender that a pin or needle would fall through. At length it will sustain a pebble, and, if winter still holds its unbroken sway, a child, a man, a crowd, a cart will follow."[1]

? Can you think of an area in which you may be growing spiritually calloused?

Psalm 95:8 (NIV) reads:

> Do not harden your hearts as you did at Meribah,
> as you did that day at Massah in the desert.

? What has the author of Hebrews done in 3:9 with the preceding quotation from Psalm 45:9?

For the place-names *Meribah* and *Massah* the author of Hebrews translates them back into their original sense: *Meribah* meaning "contention" or "strife," and *Massah* meaning "testing" or "temptation." In other words, he has understood that events in one's life can conjure up related experiences or significant memories.

Have you ever tried charting your life as geographically symbolic? This can be done in two ways: (1) start with actual significant places you've been and pinpoint the meaning of these places for you (e.g., *Oak Park* I might rename *Turning Point,* for it was there that I had to decide between someone I liked a lot who had turned away from the Christian faith, and someone I didn't like a lot but who pressed home eternal issues to me); or (2) think through your life as if it were an imaginary map and supply place-names according to significant things that have happened to you.

On the island pictured below, see if you can label a bridge (for some difficulty you had to cross over), a mountain (for some mountain-peak experience), a valley (for some low point in your life), a range of plateaus (for a stretch of ongoing activities or a job). Come up with three other made-up place names to represent your own life-experiences.

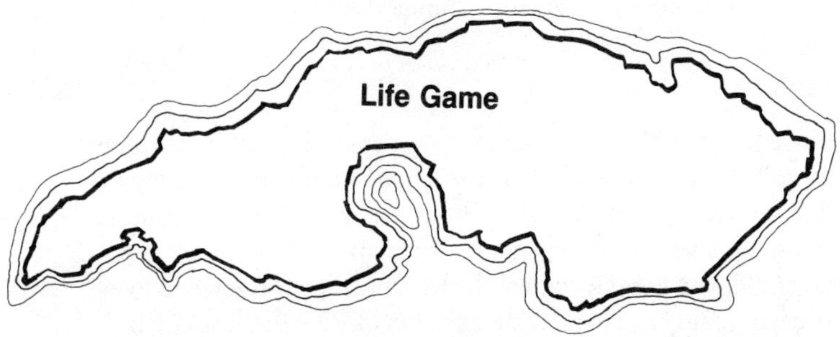

The danger depicted in Hebrews 3:12 (and constantly throughout the leter) is that of spiritual mutiny, of going A.W.O.L. from God. The danger resounds from the word *departing.* It represents the Greek verb from which we derive the word *apostasy.*

 The term *apostasy* describes a deliberate, defiant departure from the living God. The idea of apostasy is portrayed in various forms and figures in the New Testament. For example:

Luke 8:13, "Those . . . are the ones who receive the word with joy . . . . They believe for a while, but in the time of testing they fall away."

I Timothy 1:19, "Some . . . have shipwrecked their faith."

II Peter 2:21, "It would have been better for them not to have known the way of righteousness, than to have known it and then to turn their backs . . . ."

I John 2:18, 19, "Many antichrists have come. They went out from us, but they did not really belong to us . . . ."

In Hebrews this phenomenon is called:

to turn away from—God" (3:12)
to "fall away" (6:6)
to "deliberately keep on sinning after we have received the knowledge of the truth" (10:26)
to "shrink back and [be] destroyed" (10:39).

 Augustine said, "God has promised forgiveness to your repentance, but He has not promised tomorrow to your procrastination."

The "lava" continues to pour from the preacher as five molten questions erupt in verses 16-19. They are rhetorical questions, as if a mother were to say to the five-year-old, "You know better than to get into the cookies, don't you?" No answer needed.

During those 40 years of wandering the Sinai peninsula became a kind of monumental mausoleum. F. B. Meyer said picturesquely, "The sand their winding-sheet; the solitude their mausoleum."[2]

Faith Rest

Little wonder, then, that chapter 4 opens, "Therefore let us be on our guard" (Weymouth). However, the mood difference in chapters 3 and 4 is painted by F. B. Meyer: "The contrast between the third and fourth chapters of this epistle is very marked. The former is like a dreary November day, when all the landscape is drenched by a sweeping rain . . . [while] the latter is like a still clear day in midsummer when nature revels in reposeful bliss beneath the unstinted caresses of the sun."[3]

 What key word (or its negative counterpart) is found in Hebrews 3:12, 18, 19; 4:2, 3, 6, and 11?

Vance Havner classified the wilderness wanderers as spiritual window-shoppers. Once more, our preacher-author targets his hearers with the reference to "none of you" (4:1; see also 3:12). The author's New Testament readers are paralleled with the Old Testament generation, since both had good news dispensed to them (4:2).

What made the difference? Picture a chemistry laboratory. Chemicals are gurgling. The scientist is lifting two beakers. In the same way, when God's message is given to people, the difference in spiritual chemistry for some lies in that "those who heard did not combine it with faith." (The KJV has "not being mixed with faith.") Faith is the catalyst that makes the difference.

In Hebrews 4:3 the author defines *who* does enter, or *how* God's rest is entered: by faith. Note that there are various views of this section:

1. Some hold that the celestial Canaan (or our entrance to Heaven) is in view. Many of the old spirituals talk about crossing Jordan, referring to death.
2. Some believe the author is talking about an after-conversion faith rest—the sort of thing missionary Hudson Taylor

experienced upon surrendering himself to let God work through him.

3. The simplest view, based on 4:2, is that believers are enterers and enterers are believers. This is the view accepted here.

A colorful argument, evidently appealing more to ancient than to modern minds, follows in Hebrews 3:7-9. It is charted below, then explained.

Joshua (c. 1400 B.C.) (Heb. 4:8)	David (c. 1000 B.C.) (Heb. 4:7)
God offered rest	God offered rest later

Therefore, a rest remains to enter (Heb. 4:9)

The word "rest" in Hebrews 3 and 4 is a complex concept; that is, it has a multiple meaning. This term includes what we might call:

1. Creation rest (Heb. 4:3, 4);
2. Canaan rest (Deut. 12:9);
3. Christian rest;
4. Celestial rest.

His argument (charted above) runs like this: If Joshua (4:8) had provided full rest for God's people, why would David (some 400 years later) still be talking about a rest to be experienced? Therefore, a rest remains for people to enter (4:9).

Note in Hebrews 4:8 that this is one place where the King James Version has made an error (as also in Acts 7:45). *Jesus* is the Greek equivalent of the Hebrew name *Joshua* (both names meaning "the Lord saves" or "The Lord is salvation"). When we think of Jesus, we think of the Lord Jesus Christ. Therefore, virtually every modern translation (e.g., NAS, NIV, Berkeley, Williams, NKJV) will correctly insert "Joshua" into 4:8 instead of "Jesus."

At least one valuable lesson emerges from Hebrews 4:7. What was David doing? He was making the Scripture message current. He was personalizing it in the present. For some Christians the Bible is a great attic-and-mothball world of the historic fall into sin, Jericho and Jebusites, Jews and Samaritans. They have never learned to look at the Bible through the lens of life. They do not see, for example, that the Samaritan issue in the New Testament has implications for race relations today. They have never understood of the Bible: "This . . . is for you" (Mal. 2:1). On the cover of our Bible we ought to etch mentally those words—*this is for you!*

Consequently, the author of Hebrews concludes: a rest is remaining for you (Heb. 4:9). Already in Hebrews 4:2 the author defined God's rest-enterers as believers. Now here in Hebrews 4:10 he defines a rest-enterer as someone who "rests from his own work." Is this Paul's doctrine of being justified by faith and not meritorious works (see Rom. 3:26-28 and 4:1-6)?

What apparent contradiction do you spot in Hebrews 4:10 and 11, and how would you solve it?

Hebrews 4:10 says to stop working; Hebrews 4:11 exhorts us to "make every effort." (Similarly paradoxical is I Thess. 4:11, which Chester Woodring paraphrased: get all stirred up about settling down!)

The Word of God

In contrast to all those unbelieving Israelites who *died* (4:11), "the word of God is *living*" (4:12). Hebrews 4:12 is a frequent Bible verse memorized by children, but memorized out of context. What does all this description of God's Word mean in its context in Hebrews?

Can God's Word be of no value (a trick question—think about it)?

The answer to the question (properly understood) is: yes. Hebrews 4:2 says that "the message [that is, God's Word] that they [the Israelites] heard was of no value to them." An insurance policy has great value of itself, but if the beneficiary knows nothing about the policy, or refuses to use it, he or she receives no actual benefit from it. Similarly, God's priceless Word can prove to be "of no value" to us if we do not plug its power (by usage) into our situation.

The reason that the Word of God is powerful is that the God of the Word is the source and force behind the Word of God. This titanic truth comes through in verse 12 and 13, for verse 12 spotlights the Word of God, whereas verse 13 faces us with the God of the Word.

> The Word of God leads us to find the God of the Word, even as the cog-wheels on the train, and . . . the track on a Swiss railway, work the one in the other and enable the engineer to bring the train into the glorious scenery of the Alps.
>
> —F. E. Marsh, *The Greatest Book in Literature*

In the context of Hebrews 3 and 4, Hebrews 4:12 must refer back to that life-giving Word which (ironically) dealt death to the disobedient (3:17) Israelites, creating that huge Sinai cemetery. That living Word that brought the deathblow to the disobedient in the wilderness spoke again in David's day (thus, Ps. 95:7b-11).

This Word is "sharper than any double-edged sword" (4:12).

How has God's Word proved to be like a sharp, double-edged sword to you?

Arthur Miller, the playwright, said he recognized a great play when, enthralled in the midst of the play and entering emotionally into some character in the play, he irrupted with "that's me." In other words, the play had penetrated him personally. Even so, God's Word can penetrate "even to dividing soul and spirit, joints and marrow" (4:12).

DICHOTOMY OR TRICHOTOMY?

The two long words in the heading simply assert that human beings are essentially two-part (*di-*) creatures or three-part (*tri-*) creatures. Theologians debate this issue.

Trichotomists base their view mainly upon Hebrews 4:12 and I Thessalonians 5:23, which seem to dissect humanity into three compartments. Trichotomists usually hold that the spirit relates us mainly to God, while the soul relates us principally to other humans. (It is questionable, however, whether such an oversimplification can be maintained as one traces all usages of "soul" and "spirit" throughout the Bible by means of a concordance.) Theologian Augustus Strong claimed that Hebrews 4:12 meant "not the dividing of soul *from* spirit,—but rather the piercing . . . to the very depths of the spiritual nature."[4]

Dichotomists believe that the three-part scheme is too neat and won't hold water. For instance, in Mary's poetic hymn of Luke 1:46 and 47, the parallel lines

> My soul glorifies the Lord
> and my spirit rejoices in God my Savior

do not seem to support the trichotomist distinction between soul and spirit. In Luke 1 both soul and spirit are relating to God.

Still further, dichotomists argue: why stop with only three parts? Why not divide humans into four parts (on the basis of Mk. 12:30)? Besides, there are still other psychological and physical names from the Bible left unaccounted for, even by a four-compartment view. Therefore, dichotomists urge that it is simpler to understand humans in terms of a twofold material and nonmaterial makeup, inserting various names under each of these two categories.

The Word of God "judges" (4:12). This represents the Greek word from which we derive "critic." God's Word is our supreme critic.

It is said that an American visitor to a great art museum in Florence, Italy, remarked in the presence of the guide, "Are these the great masterpieces I've heard so much about? I don't see all that much in them." The guide replied, "These paintings are not on trial, sir. You are." The critic became the criticized.

Someone once said to a well-known New Testament scholar that he knew few scholars who stood upon the Word of God. To make a point the scholar replied emphatically: "I don't stand on the Word of God; I stand *under* it."

If the Word of God can penetrate so incisively, as Hebrews 4:12 claims, then the God behind that Word must have all-penetrating knowledge, as 4:13 claims: "Everything is uncovered and laid bare before the eyes of him to whom we must give account." In the apocryphal book by Jesus the Son of Sirach we read, "Their ways are always before him [God], they will not be hid from his eyes" (Ecclesiasticus 17:15).

The word translated "laid bare" (KJV: "opened") is found in Greek outside of the New Testament in several contexts. In each case it seems to refer to an inescapable exposure. For instance, it can refer to the bending backward of a sacrificial animal's neck for slaying. It also appears to be used in something like a wrestler's stranglehold on his victim, so that the opponent is powerless to move. Furthermore, it could be used of a criminal prior to execution, who has a dagger pointed upward under his throat so that it is impossible to bow his head in shame. In each of the above cases, the neck appears prominently, as *trach* (such as in our *trachea*) appears in the Greek word *tetrachelismena* for "laid bare."

The writer James Joyce achieved fame by his "stream of consciousness" style of writing. Out of his consciousness poured four-letter words, nonsense phrases, etc. Indeed, it does represent what emerges from human consciousness! Yet nothing escapes the all-X-raying consciousness of the living God.

It is this God "to whom we must give account" (Heb. 4:13). From the backdrop of bookkeeping, our author depicts God as the all-seeing Auditor to whom our accounts must be rendered. No wonder we pray, "Forgive us our debts."

The greatest thought that ever entered my mind is my personal accountability to God. —Daniel Webster

CHAPTER 5

PRIEST EXTRAORDINAIRE

Hebrews 4:14—5:10

"What's wrong with the world?" asked G. K. Chesterton, who answered, "*I'm* wrong with the world."[1] Gerard Manley Hopkins spoke of "the bent world." Therefore, ala Chesterton, I must be bent. This bentness, this out-of-kilteredness, this gone-awryness is what the Bible labels as *sin*.

If I'm wrong with the world (or, greaterly, if I'm wrong with God), who will put me right? The Bible proclaims that God has a "Rightener," one who can put this humpty-dumpty world back together again in its right order.

Here I stand—with my imperfection (called sin) before Perfection (called God). What can I do? I need a giant named *Between*—one who will be my go-between midway between a perfect God and an imperfect humanity. Throughout history people (whether rightly or wrongly) have functioned as these go-betweens. We call them *priests*. Like a telephone operator helping me get reconnected when I have a connection full of static, or have been disconnected, a priest's role is to connect me with the living God.

If you were filling out a questionnaire, detailing what kind of priest you'd like to have between you and God, what specifications would you call for?

Jesus, the Christians' Priest

Shock! Ridiculousness! Imagine the average Jewish person hearing this, the author's thesis statement (Heb. 4:14), for the first time. "Wait a minute. You're not trying to tell me this Jesus *was a priest*, are you?" might be the response. Further, "When did your Jesus ever function as a card-carrying priest in the Jerusalem Temple? When did your Jesus ever wear the gorgeous, brilliant priest's uniform in the worship ritual? When did your Jesus ever slit a lamb's throat to offer it as a sacrificial animal?"

These are all good questions that we modern Christians have probably never really pondered. Yet, they would be normal questions to a Jew being told that Jesus is a priest.

"We have a great high priest . . . Jesus the Son of God" (Heb. 4:14). This is the punch line of the midsection of Hebrews (4:14—8:5), indeed, of the whole Book of Hebrews. As a matter of fact, no other New Testament book deals explicitly with this topic. Jesus is said to do things priests do elsewhere in the New Testament (e.g., "is . . . interceding," Rom. 8:34; serves as "mediator," I Tim. 2:5), but never in other New Testament writings is this theme explored. Simon Kistemaker stated, "The term *priest* occurs 31 times in the New Testament, 14 of which appear in Hebrews. The word *high priest* is featured 123 times in the Gospels, Acts, Hebrews. The expression does not occur in the other Epistles and Revelation. In Hebrews it is used 18 times."[2] Incidentally, the fact that Paul never used the term *high priest* is another argument against seeing Paul as the author of Hebrews.

In his German translation of the New Testament, Martin Luther appropriately began a new chapter with Hebrews 4:14. Hebrews 4:14-16 is like the bull's-eye of the Book of Hebrews. Martin Luther said, "After pouring in wine into our wound [in chapters 3 and 4], he [the author of Hebrews] now pours in oil."[3] Chapter 3 especially must have burned like iodine on an open cut, but now comes the soothing medication.

After the declaration of the Son's priesthood came the deductions drawn from it, which are principally two:

1. "let us hold firmly to the faith we profess (4:14)

   and

2. "let us . . . approach the throne of grace with confidence" (4:16).

The impact of coming before deity is either distressingly heightened or cushioned, depending upon the *kind of* deity one is coming before. In the mental milieu of the New Testament world, to the Stoics God was indifferent; to many Jews God was very high and different (so again, that really made God indifferent); and to Epicureans God was untouchable.[4] As Vernon Grounds put it concerning some false models of deity, "their God is a kind of cosmic icicle, a God of unruffled serenity, a God who has an empty blank where His heart ought to be."[5] Within this conceptual crucible it must have been jolting to meet a sympathetic Savior-Priest. The two "nots" the author ties in Hebrews 4:15 result in a positive proclamation—we have a High Priest who can sympathize with our weaknesses.

Aristophanes, a Greek playwright, in *The Frogs* presents a dominant Greek idea that the divine cannot feel and suffer. In trying to decide between two travelers (which is a slave and which a god?), the advice is given:

> You should flog him well,
> For if he is a god he won't feel it.
> Whichever of us two you first behold
> Flinching or crying out—he's not the god.

By contrast, the Christian's high priest can sympathize (in the Greek, *syn* = with; *path* = feel). Who can "feel [together] with" someone except one who can *feel*—period? Jesus has possessed the same sensory capacities, the same hormones, the same retinal images that I have. He is the Understander; He is our Empathizer.

In fact, Jesus was "tempted in every way. . . we are—yet without sin" (4:15). That does not mean tempted with every conceivable specific temptation. For instance, He was obviously never tempted to take LSD or cheat on income tax forms.

The citadel of Christ's human nature underwent assault. The arrows of temptation flew around Him. Christ "was [no] mailed champion exposed to toy arrows."[6] "His soul was not hard as flint or cold as an icicle."[7]

Nevertheless, when the blazing flame of temptation lashed out toward Him, there was no "combustible material to which it could set light."[8] When the enemy hordes of temptation beseiged Him (unlike with us), there was no traitor or fifth columnist from within to open the door to the enemy.

"God made him who had no sin to be sin for us" (II Cor. 5:21).

He "was without sin" (Heb. 4:15).

"He committed no sin" (I Pet. 2:22).

"In him is no sin" (I Jn. 3:5).

Jesus was sinless so He could *solve* our sinful predicament, yet Jesus is sympathetic so He can *understand* our human predicament. Since that is the case, Hebrews 4:16 can offer a perfectly approachable God.

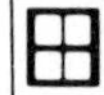

I liked Timmy. The reason I liked Timmy was that he found me approachable. The little guy bobbed over from the apartment complex next door. I don't know whether his mother hadn't told him, "Don't talk to strangers" or whether he was just outgoing. I never regarded myself as the world's most extroverted conversationalist, so it made me feel good when Timmy marched right up and began to babble. He did not find me "a hard man" (Mt. 25:24). I think God must enjoy it a lot when we approach Him as approachable.

Some years ago there was a television program called *Candid Camera.* On that show a hidden TV camera captured unsuspecting victims at their candidest. God wants us to come to Him candidly, uninhibitedly, unsuppressedly.

How could God be likened to a counselor, psychologist, or psychiatrist?

"The apostle is inviting us to view God," commented Vernon Grounds, "as though He were a kind of super-psychiatrist. As William James put it: we can exteriorize our rottenness to psychiatrists."[9] Here is a God with whom we can ventilate all our feelings and "receive mercy" (4:16).

When we are in need, we want help wedded with mercy. The patient in the infirmary does not like to be treated as a broken watch. Oh that he were at home again, to be nursed by the soft hands of his mother which always seemed so skilled and gentle and soft.

—F. B. Meyer, *The Way Into the Holiest*

Say, have you been frapped lately? "Frapped," you say, "what's that?" We will explain. Hebrews 4:16 says with God we can find grace "to help." This verb is actually a noun in Greek and would be better rendered "for [timely] help" or "resulting in appropriate help." In Acts 27:17 (the scene of Paul's shipwreck en route to Rome) we find the plural form of the same noun, being informed there that the sailers "used helps, undergirding the ship" (KJV). This seafaring process is a technical nautical term called "frapping." In the case of the ship that was about to "come unglued" (as modern people might say) the sailors tied ropes or cables around the ship's hull so as to hold the structure intact during the frenzied storm. These were the "helps," or frapping technique.

So then, have you been "frapped" lately? As if we were that storm-tossed ship, about to come apart at the seams, at times we need God's help, His frapping. As an old hymn says:

> And His cables stretched
> from His heart to mine
> Can defy the [storm's] blast
> through strength divine.

? Can you think of an occasion when you prayed and God supplied help that was more than mere coincidence?

Ω An illuminating insight comes as we turn to Mark 6:21 for another use of the same Greek word behind the expression "in time of need" (KJV). Mark 6:14-29 tells the story of Herod Antipas, Herodias the vulturess, Salome the voluptuous, and the dauntless John the Baptist, who would rather lose his head than his character. The text tells us that the sinister and scheming Herodias was waiting for "the opportune time."

In modern televiewing terms we would call this "prime time" for Herodias to act. Her action was "well-timed," tailored to the awful occasion. In the same way, many of God's prayer answers come to us like coats tailored to physique. They are matchers. They come, as we say, just in the nick of time. Just as Herodias's plot matched the horrible circumstances, God's answers so often match our times of need.

A quick outline will help us at this juncture:

I. *Declaration of and deductions from Jesus' high priesthood (4:14-16)*
II. *Description of the qualifications of any high priest (5:1-4)*
III. *Detailing of the qualifications of Jesus the High Priest (5:5-10)*

"We have a great high priest . . . Jesus the Son of God" the author asserted in Hebrews 4:14-16. This surely would have roused the rejoinder, "Huh? Jesus a priest? I don't remember your Jesus ever performing a priest's duties. Prove it!" Therefore, in Hebrews 5:1-10 the author lines out:

I. The general qualifications of all high priests (1-4) followed by
II. The specific qualifications of Jesus as High Priest (5-10).

In these two sections of Hebrews 5:1-10 there is something of an a-b-c-c-b-a pattern. In 5:1-4 the author shows how priests must have:

A. a human constitution (5:1),
B. a humane compassion (5:2, 3), and
C. a heavenly calling (5:4).

Then in Hebrews 5:5-10 ("So Christ also . . .") the author—in virtually reverse order—demonstrates how Christ possesses exactly these three credentials and, therefore, is a legitimate high priest.

A Priest's Description

If you had to define what a high priest is and does, what would you say?

Hebrews 5:1 gives us an excellent definition of a high priest's duties. Each high priest has a:

1. selection "from among men," and
2. representation "related to God," and a
3. function— "to offer . . . sacrifices for sins" (5:1; compare 8:3).

What is truly essential for priests? First, they had to have the make-up of those they represented, i.e., have human nature (5:1). Secondly, they had to have on-the-job compassion (5:2, 3).

The word for compassion ("deal gently" in the NIV) in Hebrews 5:2 is found only here in the New Testament. Many "feeling" words are formed on the *path*-root. For example,

sym-pathy (feel with)
em-pathy (feel in[side])
anti-pathy (feel against)
a-pathy (no feeling)

The Greek word in Hebrews 5:3, however, has no English equivalent. If it did, it would probably be *metripathy*. *Metr* words, such as meter, metronome, etc., deal with measuring things. This particular Greek word urges us to have just the *right amount* of feeling.

The Greek philosopher-genius, Aristotle (c. 350 B.C.) came up with the idea of a golden mean, i.e., reaching a midpoint between two extremes. Some people's emotions are like Vesuvius; others are like Old Stoneface. The golden mean between insensitivity and hyper-sensitivity would be just the right amount of sensitivity. It is a kind of emotional equator between tropical and arctic zones.

An Old Testament priest could not swing to either end of the pendulum with his emotions and still be effective. On the one hand, he could not be soft on sin (like Eli the priest was with his sons); on the other hand, he could not come out screaming, "This is the second time you've been back here today" when a sinning Israelite brought a sacrifice to the Tabernacle. *That's what he was there for.* Priests were sin specialists. Sinless people would put priests out of work.

This is a tightrope for us to walk, too, in our relationships with people. It is the tightrope of not condoning sin but not condemning the sinner. It is working toward an equipoise in our emotions—not indifferent toward sin but not indignant toward the sinner. Stoics don't make good caregivers. People don't need porcelain pharisees when they've blown it.

Can you remember a scene when you were too hard or too lenient with a fellow sinner? Can you recall an instance where someone shared your concrete compassion?

The non-Christian Bertrand Russell wrote apologetically: "There are certain things that our age needs. . . . The root of the matter is a very simple and old fashioned thing, a thing so simple that I am almost ashamed to mention it for fear of the derisive smile with which wise cynics will greet my word. The thing I mean—please forgive me for mentioning it—is love, Christian love or compassion."[10]

F. W. Boreham told of a streetcar scene in Australia one dreary winter day. An elderly woman boarded the streetcar with great difficulty. All eyes were riveted on her because she was holding a bouquet of wattle, a brilliant golden flower. Before her exodus she handed some flowers to a newsboy, who took them without a word of thanks. When she got off the streetcar, and as it was starting up again, the newsboy threw the flowers on the floor while the old woman watched, horror-stricken. F. W. Boreham dove down to rescue them, but he said that he never forgot the look on an old lady's face for the lack of a little compassion.

The reason that a high priest could—and we can—have compassion on those who fall into sin is that he was—and we are— "compassed with infirmity" (5:2, KJV). (The same Greek word translated "compassed" is used of the chain tied around Paul in Acts 28:20.)

In addition to a human constitution and humane compassion, a Jewish high priest had to have a heavenly calling (5:4). Little Jewish boys never scratched their heads and said, "I think I'd like to be a high priest when I grow up." Either you were in the priestly tribe of Levi or you weren't. If priests came to high priesthood legitimately (and many between the Old and New Testament periods didn't), they didn't do it by social climbing. No true high priest was a democratically elected official. He was a God-called person.

Does Jesus have the credentials that any and every high priest should have? The author takes pains (in 5:5-10—"So Christ also . . .") to demonstrate that one can check off these same three credentials that he laid out in 5:1-4 as being true of Jesus.

In order to show that Jesus was a God-called priest, the author cites two Old Testament texts, Psalm 2:7 and Psalm 110:4 (in Heb. 5:5 and 6). Notice that the Messiah is heralded as king in Psalm 110:1 and is hailed as priest in Psalm 110:4 (Heb. 5:6).

Once the author has established Jesus' heavenly calling to the priesthood (5:5, 6), he reverts back to His human constitution and compassion (5:7, 8). "Nowhere in the New Testament is the humanity of Christ set forth so movingly."[11]

Here in Hebrews 5:7, 8 we are given an amplified picture window view of Jesus in the Garden of Gethsemane scene beyond what we find in the four Gospels. The four Gospels do not specifically mention Jesus' "loud cries and tears" (5:7) in the Garden of Gethsemane. But Philip Hughes, commenting on this phrase in the Hebrews text, says it shows us that Jesus didn't die "a relatively pleasant death" like "Buddha Gautama in the gardens of Kusinara."[12]

Jesus' humanness became acutely apparent in His suffering. Christ "learned obedience in the school of suffering" (5:8, NEB).

Beneath the surface of the English text is a rhyming jingle in the Greek text . . . *emathen* . . . *epathen* (He learned . . . He suffered). This word-play is similar to Louis Bromfield's description of a prairie dog: "There is a perkiness, a jerkiness about him."[13]

This is the only place in the New Testament where Jesus is explicitly said to have "learned."

 Blessed are they who learn without pain—but blessed few.

—Jim Townsend

The most exacting test of the human being is in how he endures suffering.

—Pearl Buck, *The Gifts They Bring*

How could the perfect Son of God be "made perfect" (5:9)? For us to become perfect would imply previous imperfection, but not for the sinless Jesus. At their root several Greek words for perfection have *telos* (e.g., *telos* = end or goal; *phone* = sound; therefore, a *telephone* enables us to "sound" our voice to another "end or goal"). By His sinless life Jesus could reach His *telos*, or goal, to die a sinless death on behalf of the sinful. Consequently, Jesus "became the source of eternal salvation for all who ______________________________

____

Him." (What words of condition would you have followed this statement with?)

The author of Hebrews calls Christians those "who obey him [Christ]" (5:9). In fact, to believe and to obey are virtually synonymous in Hebrews. Believers are obeyers.

This brings our author back full circle to his sermon text from Psalm 110:4 in Hebrews 5:10. That will become his launching pad for an extended takeoff.

We have studied:

III. *The priesthood interposed (4:14—8:5)*
   A. The validity of His priesthood is based on official qualifications (4:14—5:10)

Now we're ready to study:

   B. The superiority of His priesthood is based on the order of Melchizedek (5:11—7:28)

CHAPTER

6

GOING ON OR FALLING AWAY?

Hebrews 5:11—6:20

He was outgoing, ardent, likable, brilliant. He had come from a family of non-Christians. He was intense about evangelizing others. He was the only student in the Bible school that I attended who took the trouble to get down on his knees and pray with me. I felt a strong emotional bond for him. I remember him rushing me out of my room one day as I was recovering from a cold and dragging me to a Chicago zoo. Jack made an indelible mark upon me.

Two years later the president of the Bible school told me, "I think Jack is an apostate." It shook me to the very core. I literally fell down the library stairs a few minutes later. I called Jack up, reported what had been said, and he met me in a nearby restaurant. I still remember him slamming his fist on the restaurant table and saying, "Only what you can see and feel is real."

Although Jack had been attending a "Christian" liberal arts college, he no longer claimed to be a Christian. How was I to explain what had happened to Jack?

How would you explain what happened to Jack? Was Jack a Christian, or not?

Read through Hebrews 5:10—7:3 to see if you can trace the author's flow of logic through this section. Then see if the drawing on the next page makes sense to you. It is as if the author bounces on a thought at Hebrews 5:10, then dives off into a pool of thought, only to swim full circle and arrive back at the very point at which he started (namely, to talk about Melchizedek).

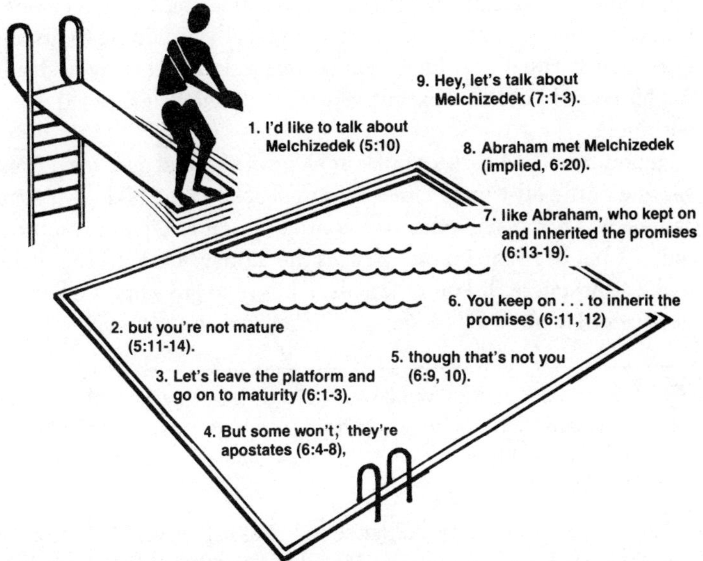

In Hebrews 5:1-10 the author had discussed:

1. The three credentials any high priest must have (1-4); and
2. the three credentials Jesus has as our High Priest (5-10).

The third of these credentials is to be God-called (5:10), which the author proves by quoting Psalm 110:4 . . . about Melchizedek.

Immaturity (5:10-14)

We might imagine the modern comic strip "light-bulb-over-the-head effect" happening to our author at 5:10. Just mentioning Melchizedek triggers in his mind the reaction that his readers aren't ready to hear about Melchizedek. Therefore, the author's *thesis* (Jesus is a priest like Melchizedek) is interrupted by a long *parenthesis* (5:11-6:20) until he arrives again to talk finally about Melchizedek.

It would be tragically amusing if some Sunday morning everyone from your church might come dressed physically according to his or her individual spiritual age. Imagine a 90 year old man coming in diapers, or a 55 year old business executive with teen hairstyle and fad clothing![1]

Hebrews 5:10-14 uses a similar analogy of spiritual age. John Riggins was one of the all-time premier running backs in the NFL. For some time he was not playing due to a contract dispute. Upon his return he said, "What did I miss most? Besides the money? I missed the little kiddie atmosphere. If I quit football, I'd have to grow up."[2] That is the message of Hebrews 5:11—6:3 . . . let's go on and grow up.

? What characteristics would you list for at least three growth levels of Christians? What spiritual age rating would you give yourself? In what one area would you say you're spiritually immature? In what area do you feel mature?

The author assessed his audience as being babies (5:12, 13), as slow learners (5:11). Given the time lapse between their coming into the Christian community and the point at which the author was writing, they ought to have been mature enough to teach others. In Hebrews 5:12 the author implies the doctrine of the teacherhood of all believers (not meaning they must become professional educators).

The earmark of immaturity is that the readers are "not acquainted with [KJV: 'unskilful in' . . . only here in the Greek New Testament] the teaching about righteousness" (5:13). This "teaching about righteousness" is most likely explained in 5:14.

Spiritual grown-ups are "those who through constant practice have their spiritual faculties carefully trained" (Weymouth) "to discriminate between what is good and what is bad" (J. B. Phillips, 5:14).

? How does Hebrews 5:14 apply to everyday life?

In these times when people pay high fees to go to a workout clinic, aerobics class, racquetball court, or gym, how many would pay a comparable fee to have a moral discernment workout? (The word "exercised" [KJV] is the Greek word from which we derive *gymnasium* and *gymnastics*). Yet, what could be more valuable to the Christian than this?

Years ago I recall seeing a very colorful biology textbook. In the book were a grouped series of plastic sheets that could be overlaid atop a picture of the human skeleton. One overlay contained the human muscles. Another transparency sheet showed the nervous system. Still another gave the "organ recital." All the colored plastic overlays together presented a composite picture of the human anatomy.

This illustration offers insight for daily Christian experience. When a problem arises in my life today, God wants me to take the principles of Scripture, like those plastic transparencies, and overlay them onto my life situation. For a given situation a particular transparency sheet will probably be applicable, whereas another plastic overlay will not. That is where developing discernment or discrimination in decision-making comes in (Heb. 5:14). In the wrenching workout of complex decision-making we form spiritual muscle and know-how. It is hard to beat the grueling trial and error of practice, practice, practice in learning this discernment.

Give one illustration of an occasion when you faced a complicated decision—when what was right or wrong wasn't so easy for you to decide.

Opportunity (6:1-3)

At Hebrews 6:1 the author begins to prescribe what they can do about the conditions diagnosed in 5:11-14. They can "leave the elementary teachings about Christ and go on to maturity" (6:1). These teachings are presumably the ABC's the author refers to in 5:12. They are (apparently three pairs):

1. Two essential elements
   a. repentance (turning away)
   b. faith (trusting in)
2. Two external badges
   a. baptisms
   b. laying on of hands
3. Two eschatological (future) expectations
   a. resurrection
   b. judgment

Why does this list not correspond in many ways to modern indispensables? Notice what stands out about this list. All of the items are Jewish doctrines that have been brought into the Christian theological framework. The original readers ran the risk of falling back into a type of Judaistic Christianity, which would likely be much more Jewish than Christian.

Probably most modern readers will have questions about what meaning should be attached to the middle pair of key doctrines. What baptisms (note the plural) did the author have in mind? Some suggest that these were Jewish ceremonial purifications. Others maintain that he is grouping Jewish washings, John's baptism, Christian baptism, etc. At any rate, baptism and "the laying on of hands" (6:2) are joined in Acts 8:16, 17; 9:17, 18; and 19:5, 6. In each of those three cases, the imposing of people's hands is linked with the imparting of the Spirit.

The author's advice is twofold—let us:

1. leave behind the basics
2. go on to maturity.

Of course, "leave" doesn't mean abandon or discard, but rather to get on with *building beyond the foundation.* It is as if an art teacher should say to her student, "It's time to leave the lines and circles." She would mean to fill in the drawings beyond the simple pencil sketches, for an artist never really "leaves" the lines and circles.

Then the author adds in 6:3, "And God permitting, we will do so." "We will do what?" we might wonder. The statement may mean, "We (meaning "I") will go on and teach you about mature subjects." Or it may mean, "We will go on to maturity if God allows (and He won't allow apostates, in the nature of the case, to do that)."

Apostasy (6:4-8)

Just as in verses 1 and 2 the author specified six building blocks in the objective foundation of "the elementary teachings about Christ," even so in verses 4 and 5 he enumerates five subjective qualities true of those he must talk about. Study the chart below; then, reread Hebrews 5:11—6:12 in light of it.

PRONOUNS TELL THE TALE

5:11-6:3	6:4-8	6:9-12
"We" (5:11)	"those" (6:4)	"we" (6:9)
"You" (5:11)		"we" (6:9)
	"they" (6:6)	"your" (6:9)
"You" (5:12)	"their" (6:6)	
"you" (5:12)	"they" (6:6)	"your" (6:10)
"you" (5:12)		"you" (6:10)
"you" (5:12)		"you" (6:10)
		"them" (6:10)
"us" (6:1)		
		"we" (6:11)
"we" (6:3)		"you" (6:11)
		"your" (6:11)
		"you" (6:12)

Whatever interpretation of this passage one adopts, one must account for the pivotal shift in pronouns. In 5:11—6:3 and 6:9-12 the first or second person plural pronoun is almost uniformly used, whereas in 6:4-8 the third person plural pronoun is employed. Apparently, the author is talking directly to his readers as a whole, with the indirect warning as an aside to any who fall in the category described in 6:4-8.

What is true of the readers in 6:4-8? Their lofty perch is elaborated in five phrases in 6:4, 5. They are pictorally described as those who:

1. were "once . . . enlightened" (possibly meaning baptized, initiated, or instructed);
2. "tasted the heavenly gift";
3. "shared in the Holy Spirit";
4. "tasted—the word of God" and;
5. (tasted) miracles "of the coming age."

Does this description mean that they were Christians? It depends upon which scholar you consult. W. E. Vine said: "There is nothing in the details in this and verse 5 but what could take place in the experience of one who was drawn to Christianity without being born again and becoming possessed of eternal life."[3] By contrast, Grant Osborne wrote, "We must say there is no more powerful or detailed description of the true Christian in the New Testament."[4] One's view of this description is undoubtedly colored by one's theological framework! The two basic approaches to theology (and to this issue) are charted below.

Calvinism	*Arminianism*
Stems from John Calvin (1509-64) of Geneva	Stems from Jakob Arminius (1560-1609) of Holland
Accepted in Reformed and Presbyterian churches	Accepted in Methodist and Wesleyan churches
Emphasizing God's will	Stressing human free will
If God has unconditionally predestinated everything (Eph. 1:11), including the salvation of the elect (Eph. 1:4), and salvation depends upon God's work, how could a true Christian lose his salvation? ("Once saved, always saved.")	If God has genuinely granted humans free will, won't He allow them to do what they truly choose to do, including departing from God (Heb. 3:12)? We must persevere to the end by His grace.

Some Support Texts

John 10:28-30; Romans 8:29-39; Eph. 1:13,14; 4:30; Phil. 1:6; Jude 24	Mt. 24:13; Lk. 8:13; I Cor. 15:2; Col. 1:23; Phil. 2:12; II Pet. 2:21, 22; Heb. 6:4-6; 10:26-29; Jude 21

VARIOUS VIEWS ON HEBREWS 6:4-6

1. Once true Christians who are now lost (George Allen Turner)
2. Professing Christians who became apostates (John Calvin)
3. "If" (6:4) means it's hypothetical (C. Spicq)
4. "Impossible" for humans, not God (Thomas Aquinas)
5. "Impossible" means "diffficult to renew again" (Erasmus)
6. "Impossible" as long as they continue in apostasy (F. Delitzsch)
7. Refers to certain sins committed after baptism (certain early church fathers)
8. Reversion to Judaism (Bernard Ramm)

The Greek word for "falls away" (6:6) is found only here in the New Testament. It must mean the same as "turns away from the living God" (3:12), "deliberately keep[s] on sinning after we have received the knowledge of the truth" (10:26), and "shrinks back" (10:38). For these people "no sacrifice for sin is left" (10:26), they "are destroyed" (10:39), and they "fall into the hands of the living God" (10:31). This is called apostasy. In the words of Luke 8:13, "They believe for a while, but in the time of testing they fall away."

The question that people of different theological persuasions wrestle with is whether that faith is real, or like that of the demons (Jas. 2:19). By their actions these apostates are:

(1) recrucifying Christ, and
(2) "subjecting him to public disgrace" (they make an ugly *paradigm* [from the Greek word] of Christ).

An agricultural analogy in 6:7, 8 illustrates the awful reality of apostasy. Showers (divine influence) fall on two soil types, but the telltale test lies not in the blessings received (6:4, 5) but in the growth demonstrated. The rains come down on both groups, but the crops come up from only one group. Therefore: "Go on and grow up!" The immature can go on and grow; apostates can't and won't.

Steadfast Solidity (6:9-20)

After the glowering, ominous thunderclouds hovering over "them" in 6:4-8, the writer shifts back again to "you" (6:9-12). (Review the thought-flow chart on page 58. Note that in speaking to the group as a whole, the author says, "we are confident of better things in your case . . . things that accompany salvation" [6:9]).

Because of the danger of becoming dropouts, the author admonishes his audience to keep on keeping on—"to show . . . diligence to the very end" (6:11).

When William Carey was informed that he didn't possess the proper academic qualifications to be a missionary to India, he rejoined, "I can plod." Indeed he could, for Carey and his colleagues were in India seven years before baptizing their first convert.

Winston Churchill is said to have delivered a four-sentence commencement address:

"Never give up.
Never give up.
Never give up.
Never give up."

For "diligence" (6:11) we need "patience" (6:12). No more are there polka-dotted zebras or cube-shaped footballs than there is instantaneous patience. There is a taffylike resiliency inherent in patience. Endurance is the evidence of earnestness. It is by "patience [we] inherit what has been promised" (6:12).

The cartoon-page light bulb once more sparkles above the author's head, for he cannot think about inheriting promises without the superb promise inheritor, Abraham. The word "promise" is found more in Hebrews than in any other New Testament book.

Referring to the Bible's "pages begemmed with divine promise," F. B. Meyer said, "Fall flat on the divine promises; cling to them as a shipwrecked sailor to a floating spar. . . . If any man living has found one promise untrustworthy, let him publish it to the world; and the heavens will clothe themselves in sackcloth, and the sun and moon and stars will reel from their seats, the universe will rock, and a hollow wind moan through creation, bearing the tidings that God . . . can lie"[5]

In one sense, Abraham received the promise (in Isaac), yet in another sense Abraham *didn't* receive the full installment of the promise (of land—Heb. 11:9, 10, 13-16). Abraham even had to buy real estate to bury Sarah's body, despite the fact that he had been promised land with huge dimensions (Gen. 15:18-21).

In Genesis 22:16, 17 (quoted in Heb. 6:14) God stooped to use a human method to get His point across. In effect, He said like a child, "Cross my heart and hope to die." Therefore, not only did God say something, but He swore that what He said was true. The One who is All Truth put Himself under oath (6:13-16).

The midsection of Hebrews seems to revolve around these sworn statements from Scripture:

(1) Psalm 95:11 / Heb. 3:11, 18; 4:3;
(2) Genesis 22:17 / Heb. 6:13-16;
(3) Psalm 110:4 / Heb. 7:21 (5:6, 10, etc.).

Thus, God became the Underliner of His own utterance—not for His sake, but for our sakes. God provided "two unchangeable things" (6:18)—His original promise plus His oath—to insure our assurance. Like refugees "we . . . have fled to take hold of the hope offered to us" (6:18).

In 1954 Billy Graham visited Sir Winston Churchill at 10 Downing Street. The inimitable veteran of World War II asked Graham, "Young man, do you have any hope?"[6] "We have . . . hope" (Heb. 6:19).

What is there about Christianity that breeds hope in you?

For the writer "this hope" materializes in his mind in the form of a rare New Testament picture—"an anchor for the soul." This metaphor is found only here in the New Testament, although literal anchors are referred to three times in that nautically encrusted chapter on Paul's shipwreck (Acts 27). Many early Christians adopted the anchor as their emblem. In the Roman catacomb of one early Christian named Priscilla, about 66 pictorial representations of the anchor have been found.[7] This is, we might say, the coat of arms of the author of Hebrews. However, it is a not-of-this-world anchor, for it does not churn through bubbling water depths to a sandy beach-floor before our ship deck. Rather this anchor invisibly claws its prongs heavenward to the thorne of God.

Will your anchor hold in the storm of life,
When the clouds unfold their wings of strife?
When the strong tides lift and the cable strains
Will your anchor drift, or firm remain?

It is safely moored, 'twill the storm withstand
For 'tis well secured by the Savior's hand;
And the cables passed from His heart to mine
Can defy that blast through strength Divine.

We have an anchor that keeps the soul
Steadfast and deep while the billows roll,
Fastened to the rock which cannot move,
Grounded firm and deep in the Savior's love.

—*Priscilla J. Owens*

Mixing his metaphors, the author of Hebrews envisions this "anchor for the soul" as intruding into "the inner sanctuary behind the curtain" (6:19) of the heavenly Tabernacle. In the Old Testament portable Tabernacle, or worship tent, an embroidered thick curtain served as a separator between its two tent compartments—the outer, rectangular Holy Place and the inner, cubical Holy of Holies. The Holy of Holies might as well have had a phosphorescent "Keep Out" sign affixed to it, for no laity ever entered beyond that curtain. In fact, even the top Jewish religious official only entered there annually (9:25). Later (10:19-22) our author will amplify upon this blockbuster, barrier-breaking event.

It is "behind this curtain [where only a high priest could proceed], where Jesus went before us . . . on our behalf" (6:19 b, 20).

The "forerunner" (6:20) is retranslated by James Moffatt as "Jesus *entered* for us *in advance.*" The Williams translation has "where Jesus has blazed the way for us." The root parts of this Greek word involve the words "run" plus "before."

William Barclay intimated that, in Greek writers outside of the Bible, this term might be used of "a scout, a member of the reconnaisance corps of an army, the advance guard who goes ahead to see that it is safe for the body of the troops to follow."[8] Like a Kit Carson foraging ahead of the wagon train, Jesus has preceded us.

Since, at the close of chapter 6, the author illustrated perseverance by Abraham the perseverer—and Abraham was the patriarch who met Melchizedek—the author has now gotten us back to the subject of Melchizedek (to whom he will devote chapter 7). Scan once more the logical flow chart on page 58. Thus, the author's parenthesis has now come full circle back to his thesis—that Jesus is a priest "in the order of Melchizedek" (6:20). Berkeley Mickelsen informs us, "The phrase 'after the order of Melchizedek' [KJV] really means 'just like Melchizedek.' "[9]

The author who once said the readers weren't able to bite into a beefy subject like Melchizedek (5:10-12) now enters on a detailed discussion (chapter 7) of how the Messiah is like this mysterious Melchizedek. Stay tuned!

CHAPTER 7

MEL WHO?

Hebrews 7:1—8:5

In Kern and Hammerstein's musical *Showboat*, the deckhand sang the unforgettable "Ol' Man River." In it he capsuled the predicament of humanity in two memorable phrases—"tired of livin, an' feared of dyin'. " Similarly, a pop group of the early 1970's, Marmolade, sang, "The world is a bad place, a terrible place to live in. Oh-h, but I don't want to die." Both of these songs edge toward two gigantic problems of the human race:

1. The sin problem ("a terrible place").
2. The death problem ("I don't want to die").

If only we had someone "holy, blameless, [and] pure" (Heb. 7:26) who "does not need to offer sacrifices . . . for his own sins" (7:27), but who could liquidate the awesome account stacked against us. If only we had someone who "lives forever" (7:24) and we could, Peter Pan-like, fly into that forever, holding on to his shirttail. The good news—the unprecedented news—is that Christians *do* have such a person—Jesus, the Ever Living One. Christ is the contemporary of the centuries. He died once-for-all and one-for-all, but He lives for all time and for us all. This is etched in the granite of Hebrews 7. He lives!

The Mysterious Melchizedek

Finding the architectural structure beneath the antique ornateness of Hebrews 7 may be a little difficult for modern readers. Some forms of argument the author uses would probably meet with a thudding "huh?" today. But we must seek to understand Bible writers on their own terms.

? Read Genesis 14:13-24 and Psalm 110. Then close your Bible and try to write out 10 items about Melchizedek.

"Melchizedek was king . . . and priest" (Heb. 7:1). If Messiah is like Melchizedek, then Messiah is king-priest. Zechariah had predicted that the Branch would "rule on his throne. And he will be a priest on his throne" (Zech. 6:13). The author of Hebrews builds his base of comparison in that Melchizedek's "name means 'king of righteousness'; then also 'king of Salem' [probably the older name for Jerusalem] means 'king of peace' "(7:2). Thus, the author of Hebrews finds comparative meaning in Melchizedek's official position and decided name.

The unusual feature is that Melchizedek is an example of a God-worshiping high priest outside the Hebrew tradition. In other words, he was a maverick. Yet, he was a "priest of God Most High" (7:1).

Denis de Beaulieu, a 29-year old French soldier in 1429, got locked in a strange house (in an Edgar Allen Poe-like story). The Sire de Maletroit decrees that Denis will marry his niece in two hours. The girl tells Denis: "I am called Blanche de Maletroit; I have been *without father or mother*—oh! for as long as I can recollect . . ."[1]

Was Melchizedek literally "without father or mother"? Some conclude from this description that Melchizedek must have been a preincarnate appearance of the Son of God (called a Christophany). However, this would go against the grain of language, for then Melchizedek would not be "*like* the Son of God" (7:3). Things merely similar are not the same.

Melchizedek was "without father or mother, without genealogy, without beginning of days or end of life" (we should undoubtedly add) as far as the Genesis record is concerned (7:3). What do we have on him? No birth certificate nor grave epitaph. No family tree register in some musty library archives. Melchizedek appears as a lone figure on the historical horizon and then vanishes from the scene. With so little data, what shall we make of him? This much—that HE LIVES. That much we can safely affirm of Melchizedek—he lived. As far as the Biblical record is concerned, he lives. (And that will become the pulpit-pounding point for the author of Hebrews.)

The text does not say that Jesus was formed to resemble the much-earlier Melchizedek, but that the historically earlier figure (Melchizedek) was "made to resemble the [historically later] Son of God" (Berkeley Version). What might we learn from God's patterning plan?

If we may illustrate crudely with an engraving tool or tattoo-style branding iron, it was as if God had fashioned his engraving tool (the historical outline of the Son of God) first, then patterned Melchizedek's points of comparison on that pattern, even though Melchizedek stepped onto the stage of history first.

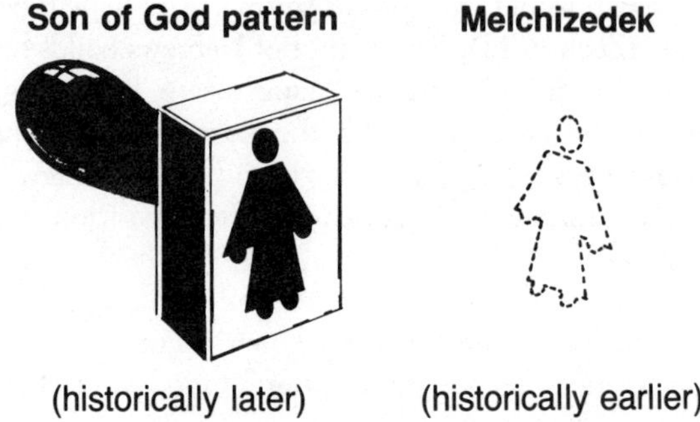

Bible students call this subject *typology.* There are people, objects, and events in the Old Testament that prefigure their counterparts in the New. For instance, just as Melchizedek *apparently* was without end of life, even so God's Son is *actually* without end. Therefore, Melchizedek is a *type* of Christ. Something about Melchizedek foreshadows something about what Jesus would be like.

The author of Hebrews argues this point not from what Scripture says, but from Scripture's silence. John Ruskin said, "There is no music in a rest, but there is the making of music in it." And Boyle stated, "The Scripture is like a dial in which we are informed by the shadow as well as the light."[2] Thus, just as pauses affect music and shadows affect sundials, the silence of Scripture is also significant.

Remarkable Reasoning

The author argues from:

1. logic and lineage (7:4-8), then from the
2. line of Levi (7:9, 10).

Behold! One greater than Abraham is here!

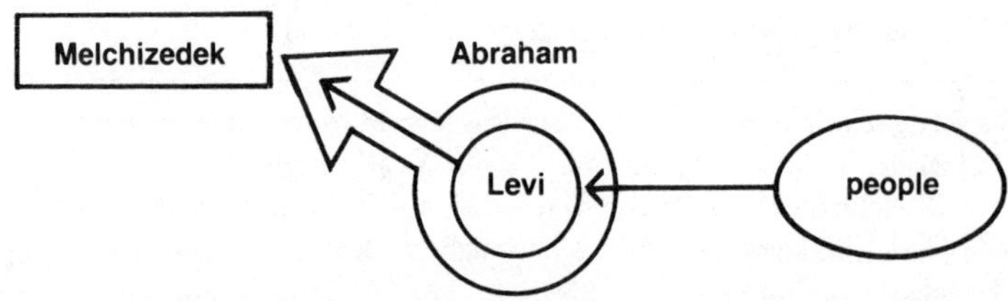

The line of logic in 7:4-10 is as follows:

1. Israelites paid tithes to Levi (that is, the Levites, or priests);
2. Levi (as if inside Abraham) paid tithes to Melchizedek;
3. Therefore, Melchizedek is greater than Levi (and the priestly order of Melchizedek is greater than that of Aaron).

The author's underlying axiom jumps out in Hebrews 7:7—"the lesser person is blessed by the greater." If people give tithes to priests, and priests bless the people, then the priests are greater than the people. The bless*er* is greater than the bless*ee*.

Battle cries! Shrieks of pain! Wounds in living color! It was four ancient kinglets versus five kings in Genesis 14. One of the five was the king of Sodom, where Abraham's nephew lived. Lot was captured. Enter, Abraham! Abraham and his 318 trained men recaptured Lot. Consequently, there was battle booty to boot. To this unprecedented priest-king (Melchizedek) Abraham "gave . . . a tenth of everything" (Gen. 14:20). This giving-and-receiving by Abraham to Melchizedek, according to the ancient customs, marked Melchizedek as the greater ("Just think how great he was" 7:4).

Under Old Testament protocol both the tither (the people) and the tithee (the priests) are Abraham's offspring. Yet one group gives tithes compulsorily to another group. Without legislated compulsion, Abraham volunteered "a tenth of the plunder" (7:4) to Melchizedek, who "did not trace his descent" from Abraham.

The author thought in terms of an ancient Near Eastern principle of solidarity. Even though Levi (from whom the priestly tribe of Levi takes its name) lived several hundred years after Abraham, the author thought of Levi as embodied in Abraham his ancestor.

Everyone "is an omnibus with his ancestors as inside passengers."
—Ian Macpherson, *God's Middleman*

Therefore, on the principle of solidarity, it was as if Levi (inside Abraham) were paying tithes to Melchizedek.

Jesus Like Melchizedek

Ever since Hebrews 5:10, the author has been asserting that Jesus is like Melchizedek. Now in Hebrews 7:11-28 he informs us how Jesus is like Melchizedek (and unlike Aaron and that pedigree of priests).

There is no successor in Christ's case (like Melchizedek)—7:11-25; there is no sacrifice needed for his own sins (unlike Aaron and sons)—7:26-28. The hinge and hub of the author's argument crops up in Hebrews 7:11, 12. By implication, it overturns the entire old order.

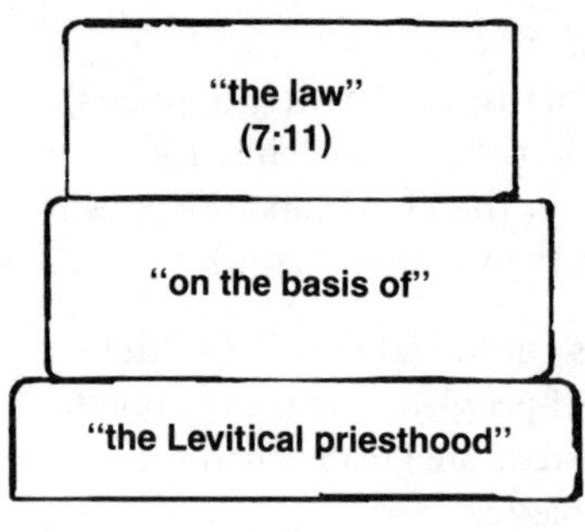

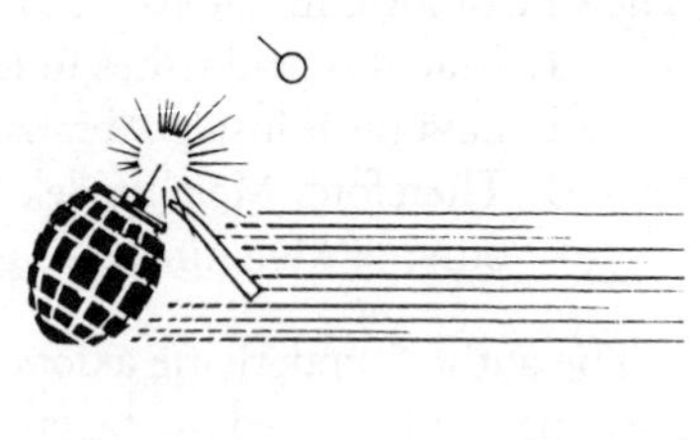

"Jesus is the Christian's great High Priest" is the author's thesis (4:14; 8:1). But any Jew would have irrupted, "But He wasn't even from the right tribe. He is disqualified to be a priest!" Of course, our author acknowledges this cardinal objection (see 8:4)—that Jesus was from the tribe of Judah, and not from the tribe of Levi (7:13, 14).

The opponent still has to explain Psalm 110:4, our author's sermon text. Why would God, around 400 years after He had instituted the Levitical priesthood, be calling for a different line of priesthood—an eternal one at that?

The most important Melchizedek-like quality Jesus possesses is "the power of an indestructible life" (7:16). Said Grady Davis, "His eternity transcends all the mutations of time, cancels all tenses except the *now* of God."[3] The "Holy One [did not] see [i.e., experience] decay" (Ps. 16:10). Unlike the automatically self-destructing tape in *Mission Impossible,* His is the "power of an indestructible life" (an expression only found at Heb. 7:16 in the New Testament).

The author seems to say that the decline and fall of the Old Testament priesthood and Law are interconnected. J. B. Phillips renders Hebrews 7:18, "Quite plainly, then, there is a definite cancellation of the previous commandment." (The term translated "cancellation" is found in the New Testament only here and in Heb. 9:26.) Undoubtedly the Jew who knew Exodus 29:9 ("The priesthood is theirs by a lasting ordinance") would have trouble stomaching the statement in Hebrews. Yet, here is God the Supplanter. Just as the Lord of the Sabbath has power over the Sabbath (Mk. 2:28), even so the Lord of the priesthood has power over the priesthood. Imagine a Jewish priest's reaction to our author calling the "former regulation" about priests (7:18) "weak and useless." This is especially inflammatory in that the Greek term for "useless" was used in the Septuagint (the Greek translation of the Hebrew Old Testament) to describe pagan idols. Get that! The function of the priesthood on a par with idols!

A. B. Bruce called Hebrews 7:19 "the dogmatic center of the

Epistle."[4] As the NIV indicates, the first part of verse 19 is in parenthesis ("for the law made nothing perfect"). In that case, eliminate the parenthesis and read straight through: "The former regulation is set aside because it was weak and useless . . . and a better hope is introduced, by which we draw near to God" (7:18, 19).

THE "BETTER"S IN HEBREWS

Better name (1:4)
Better thing[s] (6:9; 11:40)
Better hope (7:19)
Better covenant (7:22; 8:6)
Better sacrifices (9:23)
Better possessions (10:34)
Better country (11:16)
Better resurrection (11:35)
Better word (12:24)

Count the appearances of the word "oath" in Hebrews 7:20-22, 28. The Levitical priesthood was based on God's Law; the Melchizedekan priesthood is based on God's oath. The oath was both later and greater. Actually, for the first time Psalm 110:4 (see 5:6; 6:20; 7:17, 21) is quoted in its fullest form by Hebrews's author (here in Heb. 7:21).

I Maccabees 14:41 states: "And the Jews and their priests [of the inter-testamental period] decided that Simon [the last son of Mattathias] should be their leader and high priest for ever, until a trustworthy prophet should arise." Perhaps those Jews were wistfully wanting a fulfillment of Psalm 110:4 ("a priest forever").

Ω The Greek word translated "surety" by the King James Version and "guarantee" by the New International Version is found only at Hebrews 7:22 in the New Testament. This term was derived originally from the Greek word for "hand," so that what was "in the hand" was guaranteed. In extra-Biblical sources we find the word used for a person who acts as a kind of cosigner—willing to pay someone's banking debt, or post bail for a prisoner.

Augustus Toplady penned:

Thou wast Thyself our Surety
In God's redemption plan.
In Thee His grace was given us,
Long 'ere the world began."

Charles Wesley declared:

Before [God's] throne my Surety stands,
My name is written on His hands.

One of the crucial ideas in Hebrews appears for the first time explicitly in 7:22—"a better covenant." The word "covenant" (9:15, 18, 20; 10:16, 29; 12:24; 13:20; or it is in some places translated "testament") refers to God's arrangement with His people. The word is found more frequently in Hebrews (seventeen times) than in any other New Testament book.

Under the Old Covenant "there were many . . . priests, since death prevented them from continuing in office" (7:23). Like a champion rifle marksman, Death shot down those priests as if they were mechanical, parading ducks in an amusement park shooting gallery. Josephus states that there were eighty-three high priests from Aaron to the destruction of the Temple.[5]

In the case of the Christian's High Priest, Jesus, no such office-turnover is inevitable. Indeed, "because Jesus lives forever, he has a permanent priesthood" (7:24).

Jesus "always lives to intercede" for us (7:25). J. Wilbur Chapman told a story about a friend of his who knew Abraham Lincoln's son Robert. This friend had volunteered to serve in the Union forces during the Civil War. When Robert Lincoln found out that his friend was fighting on the front lines, he told an acquaintance, "When you see him, tell him . . . I will intercede with my father, the Commander-in-Chief, and perhaps I can get him something better as far as the army is concerned." Later, that same friend was to tell Chapman, "I never took advantage of the offer, but you have no idea what a comfort it was to me. Often after a weary march I would throw myself on the ground and say, 'If it gets any worse or gets beyond my endurance, I can just write to Bob Lincoln, and get relief, and I would rather have his intercession than that of the entire Cabinet, because he is the president's son.' "[6] Similarly, Jesus intervenes on our behalf.

The Amplified New Testament renders Hebrews 7:26 effectively: "[Here is] the High Priest [perfectly adapted] to our needs." Jesus is a custom fit for us. He fills the bill admirably. The match between His ability and our disability is like a custom-fit suede glove on our hand.

Our High Priest is (7:26):

1. holy (as in Acts 2:27);
2. stainless (only here and Rom. 16:18 in the New Testament);
3. pure;
4. apart from sinners (though never remote or antiseptically aloof);
5. above the heavens.

A Perplexing Problem

At Hebrews 7:27 we hit upon a perplexing problem that seems to have no simple solution. The problem is that the Old Testament doesn't really say the high priest offered *daily* sacrifices. One's response to this issue pivots upon one's view of the inspiration of Scripture. Those who hold that the Bible contains errors will simply say, "Here's one." Those who hold otherwise will suggest possible solutions and suspend final judgment.

Some point to the daily morning and afternoon burnt offerings (Num. 28:1-8), although the text does not specifically mention the high priest's involvement. In Leviticus 1:3-9 the burnt offerings presented by priests "make atonement" for individuals (1:4). The author's contemporary, the Jewish scholar Philo of Alexandria, speaks of the high priest as offering prayers and sacrifices "day by day" and, according to the Jerusalem Talmud the high priest could officiate at the daily sacrifices at his discretion during the year. Certainly, inadvertent sinning by the high priest could open the door for the high priest to sacrifice sin offerings (see Lev. 4:3ff.). Hence, there is certainly available data to substantiate the general point of the author of Hebrews here.

But imagine for a moment this scenario. The high priest in his gorgeous garments and turban approaches the altar. Suddenly he flings himself on the flaming altar, sacrificing his own body! Strange scene indeed!

Yet here in Hebrews is just such a scene. Our High Priest, Jesus, "offered himself" (7:27) as a sacrifice for sins on the altar of the cross. Such a statement would have had an air-hammer jolt for its original readers.

Priests offered sacrifices, but priests didn't offer themselves *as* sacrifices. Yet our High Priest pulls off this stunning feat! This self-offering of Christ becomes a key argument in 9:11-28.

Here It Is!

Lookout Mountain is in the area of Chattanooga, Tennessee. Its curvy, mountainside highways are quite memorable for drivers. Somewhere along those curves one begins to encounter road signs at intervals that read: "See the giant Gila Monster at the Jungle," "See the bone-crushing Python at the Jungle," etc. After passing what appears to be a wooden fortlike enclosure, you read another sign saying: "Turn around and go back. You missed the Jungle." If you were to shift into reverse and follow that instruction, you would wind up at a huge sign: "This is it: the Jungle."

Along the highway of Hebrews, we have been getting tip-off signs. Now it is as if, in Hebrews 8:1, the author says, "This is it. This custom-made description of our High Priest is found in Jesus." F. F. Bruce paraphrases, "What all this amounts to, what it all leads up to, is this." The older Miles Coverdale translation had, "This is the pyth." This is the bull's-eye of the book.

The focal point of Hebrews is that Christians have a High Priest in Jesus who is tailored to our need—and this High Priest is sitting where you'd expect a king to be sitting ("at the right hand . . . of the Majesty in heaven," 8:1; see 1:3; 4:14-16). The word "Majesty" in Greek is found only at Hebrews 1:3, 8:1; and Jude 25.

A Copyist of Plato and Philo?

In Hebrews 8:2 and 5 an issue pops up that requires some discussion. The author envisions Christ in "the sanctuary, the true tabernacle" (8:2). In fact, the Old Testament Tabernacle is called "a sanctuary that is a copy and shadow of what is in heaven" (8:5). This language coincides with language and ideas in the Greek philosopher Plato (c. 427-347 B. C.) and the Alexandrian (Egypt) Jewish philosopher Philo (c. 20 B.C.—A.D. 50), who imported Plato into Moses (and claimed Plato really got his ideas from Moses). The question, then, is whether the author of Hebrews had borrowed thought and terminology from these two thinkers. If so, it might lend further weight to the idea of Apollos as Hebrews's author, since both Philo and Apollos (Acts 18:24) were from Alexandria.

Plato told a story of a cave. A group of people were sitting in the cave facing the same direction. Behind the sitters was a fire that projected shadows onto the wall in front of them. Since the watchers were unaware of the objects casting the shadows on the cave wall, they became convinced that the shadows themselves were real.

Plato believed that our visible world was but a shadowy reflection of the true world. The real world (that we see) is but a copy and shadow (compare Heb. 8:5) of the ideal world (that we don't see). In a sense Philo the Alexandrian was the Jewish version of Plato. Therefore, it is the claim of Bible scholar H. A. Guy, "In particular, he [the author of Hebrews] adheres to Plato's theory of 'ideas'—that earthly things are but a copy of the real, eternal things in the heavenly realm."[7]

Despite the similarity in language, the fact is that the Greek version of the Old Testament, our author's Bible, contained this language long before and without resorting to Plato or Philo. For instance, note:

"See that you make them according to the pattern shown you on the mountain" (Ex. 25:40 quoted in Heb. 8:5),

or

"Set up the tabernacle according to the plan shown you on the mountain" (Ex. 26:30).

These verses, however, do not necessarily mean that the Tabernacle was a scale model of some realistic master model in Heaven. They may simply mean that Moses followed God's directions.

In Hebrews 8:5 and 10:1 the author says that these tangible, visible objects, so endearing to the Jews, were not enduring, but "shadow[s] of the good things" coming in Christ. Hence, the readers must move emotionally beyond "shadowland" (a C. S. Lewis word).

I marvel at the shadows,
    which each day and night I see.
Their thousand shapes and sizes
    never cease to interest me.
I know there's nothing to them,
    yet it always seems to me,
that every single one of them
    reflects reality.
        —in R. G. Lee, *Seven Swords*

"When [John Henry] Newman died they erected a statue to him, and on the pedestal of it are the Latin words: *Ab umbris et, imaginibus ad ventatem*. 'Away from the shadows and the semblances to the truth.' "[8]

This is the author's contention—a difficult pill for Jews to swallow—that all of the dramatic pageantry, incomparable Temple (see Lk. 21:5), priestly robes, etc., were like a gigantic version of a children's silhouette show. Now it was time to pack away the shadow-show equipment and get on with growing up!

CHAPTER

8

BLOOD COVENANT

Hebrews 8:6—9:28

Have you ever wrestled with the complexities of deciding upon insurance polices? One of the most important points of concern for anyone in such a position is: what are the benefits for the beneficiary? In Hebrews 8:6-13 God has sponsored an excellent "Insurance Policy" for His people. This group policy has both an excellent basis and excellent benefits.

The strategic, introductory words in verse 6 serve as a bridge across a canyon (compare "but now" at the outset of Rom. 3:21-26 with Rom. 3:9-20).

God's "New Covenant" Insurance Policy has an excellent basis in that it rests upon a better Covenant mediator (Jesus) and is enacted upon "better promises" (8:6). For the first time in Hebrews the term "mediator" occurs (see also 9:15; 12:24; I Tim. 2:5). It refers to someone who gets in the "middle" between others to settle some situation.

 Do you think the Old Testament Law or Covenant failed?

Enter God the Faultfinder. It might seem that there was something "wrong with that first covenant" (8:7). Indeed, the King James Version ("finding fault with them," 8:8) makes it sound like the first Covenant was defective merchandise. However, the NIV specifies that the problem was in "the people" (8:8). This viewpoint coincides with Paul's treatment of the Law in Romans 7:7—8:4. Paul raised the question, "Is the law sin?" (Rom. 7:7). He replied immediately, "Certainly not" (7:7). Later, Paul went on to explain that "the law was . . . weakened by the sinful nature" (8:3) of the human beings using the Law.

Hebrews 8:8-12 quotes Jeremiah 31:31-34—the longest quotation of an Old Testament passage in the New Testament. Again our author selects a sermon text to massage.

GOD'S 'NEW' INSURANCE POLICY

Basis: Jesus the Go-Between; better promises

Benefits

1. Internalizing God's Law (8:10a)
2. Intimacy with God (8:10b)
3. Inclusiveness of Knowledge (8:11)
4. Impartation of forgiveness (8:12)

Beneficiary: ______________________

Better Stipulations (8:6-13)

This New Covenant contains four attached benefits (see drawing above). The first benefit is the internalizing of God's character inside the human heart. In contrast to the stone slabs from Sinai—which promoted *external* motivation—the new arrangement fosters *internal* motivation. As God's "fingers" (Dan. 5:5) wrote on the walls at Belshazzar's banquet, so God's desires are etched into the fabric of Christian character ("write them on their hearts" 8:10). New

Testament popularizer William Barclay told about a deathbed incident with a former New Testament professor of his. The old Scottish highlander who had spent 17 years with his younger companion said, "Willie, when I die they'll find your name written on my heart."[1] Just as Barclay's affection was "written" on the elder Scotsman's heart, so God inscribes His very nature into the believer's being.

Secondly, an intimate interrelationship exists between God and His people (8:10b). The vow of Exodus 6:7; 19:6; Leviticus 26:12; Jeremiah 7:23; Hosea 2:23; and Zechariah 8:8 finds its fondest and final fulfillment in Revelation 21:3. Each believer can xerox Thomas's exclamation, "My Lord and my God" (Jn. 20:28).

Thirdly, inclusiveness (rather than exclusiveness) of the knowledge of God will be the order of the day (8:11). There is no lockout on the laity (Isa. 54:13). Understanding God's ways is not the monopoly of any professional group. The readers would particularly need this in light of the collapse of the priesthood in A.D. 70.

Fourthly, the impartation of forgiveness is promised (8:12). Imagine, an all-knowing God with amnesia! All of the deficits, the demerits, that were multiplying against us have been whisked away in God's great subtraction system of the cross of Christ. The cross is the plus sign that subtracts all our amassed minuses.

After he sandwiched the quote from Jeremiah into Hebrews 8:8-12, the author drew out an implication in 8:13. "New" implies "old." And what do we do with something obsolete—say, a typewriter? We discard what is obsolete and replace it with a newer model. For the Jew this audacious assertion (8:13) had staggering implications! This is not merely, as it were, the changing of the guard; this is the fall of the Bastille, the end of an era.

Some scholars feel—from Hebrews 8:13 and similar verses that speak of priestly routine and sacrificial operations in the present tense—that this implies a date prior to, but hovering around, A. D. 70—when Jerusalem was destroyed, the Temple was demolished, and the Jewish sacrificial and priestly system was forever abandoned. However, Robert Gundry noted that writers after A. D. 70 (e.g., Clement, Justin Martyr, the Jewish Talmud) still continued to use the present tense when speaking of the Jewish ritual.

Hebrews 9:2-5 is a commentary upon the "earthly sanctuary" of 9:1, and in it the author acts as our tour guide within the Old Testament Tabernacle. Read Hebrews 9:2-5 (and Ex. 25—27 and 30:1-10) and scan the sketch of the Tabernacle on the next page to get an overview of the set-up and positioning of the furniture in the Israelites' portable worship structure.

DETAIL VIEW OF TABERNACLE INTERIOR

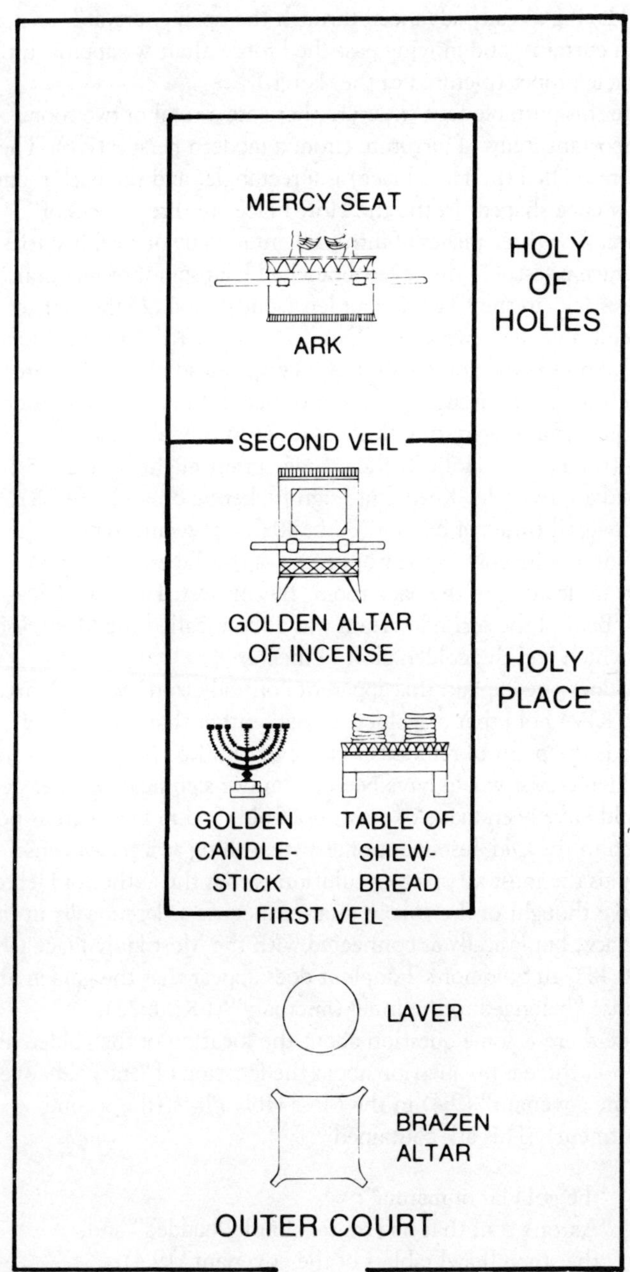

Better Sanctuary (9:1-10)

Let's do a walk through of the Tabernacle as if we were an on-duty priest. Having already advanced through the open courtyard, enclosed by linen curtains, and moving past the bronze altar, we approach the Tabernacle proper (pictured in the sketch).

Inside this portable tent structure there are a total of two rooms and four important items of furniture (from a modern perspective). The first room (called the Holy Place) is a rectangle, and the back room is perfectly cube shaped. In the the Holy Place are three pieces of furniture. The three pieces of furniture entail daily or weekly duties for the average priest: (1) the seven-branched lampstand, or menorah ("candlestick" in the KJV) to your left (south); and (2) the table of the Presence (table of shewbread in Exod. 25:23-30, KJV) to your right (north); and (3) the golden altar of incense ahead of you. You are approaching these through an east entrance in the two-room tent.

On the curtain separating the first room in the tabernacle from the second (the Holy of Holies), the average priest might have almost imagined an invisible "Keep Out" sign flickering on and off (9:8).

The overall thrust of Exodus (30:6; 40:5, 26) seems to place the golden altar of incense in the front room of the Tabernacle right before the curtain leading to the back room. By contrast, Hebrews 9:3, 4 states, "Behind the second curtain was a room called the Most Holy Place, which had the golden altar of incense."

How does one explain this apparent contradiction? Some (Martin Luther, KJV) hold that a "golden censer" rather than the altar of incense is the point of reference. However, Philip Hughes noted that any golden censer would have been of "minor significance." Besides, "it would have been made of brass, not gold, and in fact there is no mention in the Old Testament of any such thing as a *golden* censer."[2]

Perhaps the most satisfactory solution is that the author of Hebrews may have thought of the golden altar of incense as *locationally* in the Holy Place, but *logically* as connected with the Most Holy Place (see Lev. 16:13). In Solomon's Temple it does appear that the golden altar of incense "belonged to the inner sanctuary" (I Ki. 6:22).

While there is some question about the location of the golden altar of incense, there is no question about the location of "the gold-covered ark of the covenant" (9:4) in the Most Holy Place (the second compartment). This ark contained:

(1) "the gold jar of manna";
(2) "Aaron's staff that had [miraculously] budded" and;
(3) "the stone [Law] tablets of the covenant" (9:4).

The mercy seat, or "atonement cover" (9:5) was a golden lid atop the Ark of the Covenant. Above it was the centralized, localized, perfect presence of God. Beneath it were the tablets of Law, symbolizing human imperfection. Between the symbols of a perfect God and an imperfect humanity stood the mercy seat—the in-between object.

The only other place in the Greek New Testament where this word for "mercy seat" (KJV) appears is Romans 3:25 ("propitiation," KJV, or "a sacrifice of atonement," NIV). In Romans 3:25 God presents Christ as the New Testament equivalent of the mercy seat—the locus of atoning sacrifice. Hymn writer Robert Robinson testified of Jesus:

> He, to save my soul from danger
> Interposed this precious blood.

"Inter" (between) + "posed" (put, from Latin) captures admirably the in-between positioning of the mercy seat.

> There is a place where Mercy sheds
> The oil of gladness on our heads;
> A place than all beside more sweet—
> It is the blood-stained mercy seat.
> —Hugh Stowell

CHART OF CONTRASTS

Daily serving in the outer section of the Tabernacle by the regular priests	Annual service in the inner section of the Tabernacle by the high priest
The external, involuntary repeated sacrifice of animals	The essential, voluntary, unrepeatable sacrifice of Christ

The official Old Testament operation "is an illustration [literally, a 'parable'] for the present time" (9:9). The Tabernacle was God's teaching tool, His dramatized visual aid for the people.

How may God use the events and circumstances around you as a teaching tool?

The in-and-out walkathon into the first compartment of the Tabernacle for service was part of the priests' daily duties (9:6). But into the specially sacred second compartment the *high* priest went:

(1) alone;
(2) annually;
(3) accompanied always by blood (9:7).

The broadcast that the Holy Spirit was trying to beam from this whole Tabernacle pageant (9:8) was that as long as the old order went on operating, the message was: "Keep Out" of this "Top Secret" compartment. The way to God was barricaded. All the Old Testament external pageantry was "only a matter of food and drink and various ceremonial washings—external regulations applying until the time of the new order" (9:10).

Better Sacrifice (9:11-28)

Ω The expression translated "the new order" by the NIV is found only here in the New Testament. Part of the word is *orthosis*, from which we get *ortho*dontist, *ortho*podist, etc. All these words have to do with "straightening" something out. In the new order, God has thoroughly straightened things out.

Hebrews 9:11-14 is the first detailed statement in the book laying out the nature of Christ's atoning sacrifice. Throughout this section there is repeated emphasis on the "once"-ness of Christ's offering of Himself. Eight of the fifteen New Testament uses of the Greek word for "once" are found in Hebrews. The Greek word in 9:12 is actually a compounded form of "once," meaning "once for all." These words characterize the crosswork of Christ as unrepeatable and final.

Not all the blood of beasts,
On Jewish altars slain;
Could give the guilty conscience peace,
Or wash away its stain.

But Christ, the heavenly Lamb,
Took all our sins away,
A sacrifice of nobler name
And richer blood than they.
—Isaac Watts

In Hebrews 9:13, 14 the author used an argument from the lesser to the greater ("how much more," 9:14). The Old Testament high priest entered God's presence on the basis of animal sacrifices, but the Christian's High Priest entered God's presence on the basis of His own self-sacrifice. Christ "through the eternal Spirit [in Greek there is no capital letter here, so this 'S' is an interpretation] offered himself unblemished to God" (9:14). Thus, the reference may be to the Holy Spirit—the third Person of the Trinity—or to "[His] eternal Spirit [His own preexistent divine personality]" (The Amplified Version).

The "conscience" crops up for the first time here in Hebrews. The word itself is never found in the Old Testament.

Like most Bible words, this one has no formal definition contained in Scripture itself. "Nowhere in the New Testament is there a clearly defined doctrine of conscience, or even a description of it."[3] Functionwise, the conscience either accuses or excuses (Rom. 2:15). Like a meter measuring the speed of a thrown baseball, the conscience functions as a moral meter and monitor. It gives us a reading on how the rightness or wrongness of our actions stacks up against our own moral standards ("you're okay"; "you're not okay"). However, Jiminy Cricket's guideline ("Let your conscience be your guide") is not necessarily accurate, for it depends on whether our moral meter is clicking away correctly. If peoples' "consciences have been seared as with a hot iron" (I Tim. 4:2), naturally their consciences will not guide them correctly. Just as clocks have to be adjusted to correct time, even so must our consciences be aligned with the standards of God's Word.

Conscience is "the knife-edge that all our values press upon us whenever we are acting . . . contrary to those values."

—Gordon Allport, *The Individual and His Religion*

"Conscience is an ideal Moses, and thunders from an invisible Sinai."

—Augustus Strong, *Systematic Theology*

NO FORGIVENESS 'WITHOUT'

In Hebrews 9:15-17 the KJV generally uses "covenant." Covenants are prominent in Old Testament history (with Noah, Abraham, Moses, David, etc.). "In Old Testament times there does not seem to have been in existence among the Hebrews the practice of disposing of one's goods by means of a last will and testament."[4] Hence, Hebrew culture was dominated by the covenant concept, where God initiated and entered into a specified arrangement with His people.

In contrast with Jewish thought is the Greek culture. William Barclay concluded after a survey of Greek literature: "In all normal Greek in all ages *diatheke* means, not a 'covenant,' but a 'will.' "[5] The Book of Hebrews uses this Greek word more than all the other New Testament books combined.

In Hebrews 9:15-17 (and probably also Gal. 3:15-17) the idea of "covenant" gradually glides over into the notion of a last will and testament (especially Heb. 9:16, 17). Believers are beneficiaries of God's "testament" "because a will is in force only when somebody has died" (9:17)—and Christ has.

It is a smooth shift from the discussion of death in 9:16, 17 to the theme of "blood," found 6 times in 9:18-22. Exodus 24:1-8 furnishes the author's underpinnings for the account in Hebrews 9:19-21. However, numerous ingredients in 9:19 (calves, "water, scarlet wool and branches of hyssop [a plant used like a brush]," "sprinkled the scroll") are not specified at all in the Exodus account. We must assume here that the author culls these materials from a reliable extra-Biblical source.

The fundamental premise of our author is Leviticus 17:11 ("It is the blood that makes atonement for one's life"). The author of Hebrews concludes: "Without the shedding of blood [a Greek phrase he may have coined himself] there is no forgiveness."

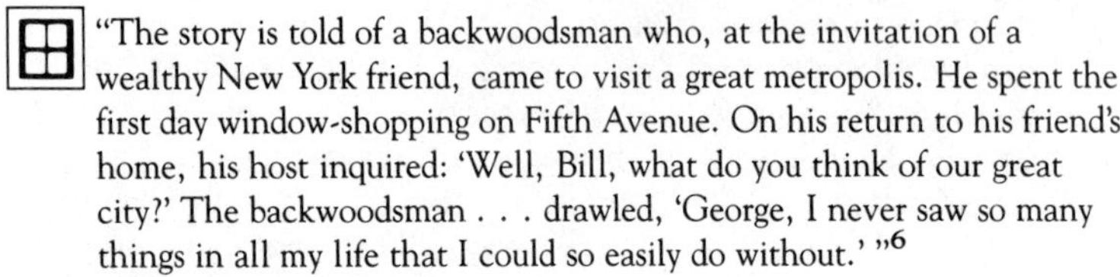

"The story is told of a backwoodsman who, at the invitation of a wealthy New York friend, came to visit a great metropolis. He spent the first day window-shopping on Fifth Avenue. On his return to his friend's home, his host inquired: 'Well, Bill, what do you think of our great city?' The backwoodsman . . . drawled, 'George, I never saw so many things in all my life that I could so easily do without.' "[6]

A superior sacrifice is one thing we cannot do without. Thus, Hebrews 9:23-28 is the very lifeblood of the whole book. As in Hebrews 9:1-11 the author portrayed the earthly sanctuary (the Tabernacle) as a sort of miniature of the heavenly sanctuary, so here in 9:23 he portrays the earthly sacrifices as scale models, as it were, of the vastly superior sacrifice of Christ. Note the three appearances of Christ: present (9:24), past (9:26), future (9:28). The Christian's Great High Priest contrasts with Old Testament counterparts at numerous points:

OLD TESTAMENT PRIESTS	*OUR GREAT HIGH PRIEST*
They entered "a man-made sanctuary" (9:24)	"he entered heaven itself" (9:24)
They offered "again and again" (9:25)	"Christ was sacrificed once" (9:28)
They entered "with blood—not [their] own" (9:25)	Christ "offer[ed] himself" (9:25)

God's great SUBTRACTION SYSTEM aims "to do away with sin" by Christ's sacrifice (9:26). It was a once-for-all offering, being both perfect and permanent.

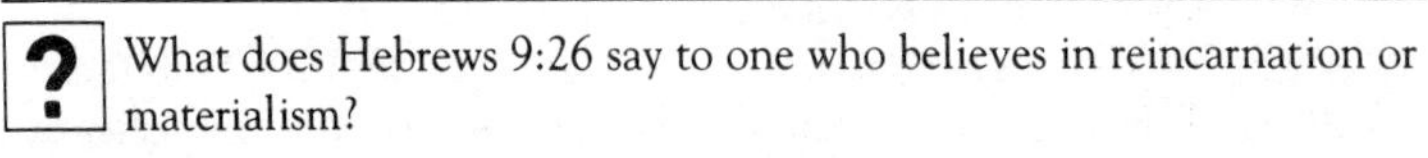

What does Hebrews 9:26 say to one who believes in reincarnation or materialism?

When earth once drinks the blood of a man, there is death once and for all and there is no resurrection.

—*The Greek writer Aeschylus*

To the proponent of reincarnation the author of Hebrews says we are "destined to die once" (agreeing with the first part of Aeschylus's quote). To the proponent of materialism the author of Hebrews says there is life beyond death ("after that . . . judgment"), disagreeing with the last part of Aeschylus's quotation. II Esdras 7:69 in the Apocrypha also speaks of "judgment after death."

The same Christ who "appeared once for all . . . to do away with sin" (9:26) "will appear a second time, not to bear sin, but to bring salvation" (9:28). As Oscar Cullmann put it, "V" Day will crown "D" Day.[7]

The Old Testament priest:
(1) offered a sacrifice for sins;
(2) was out of sight in the sanctuary; and
(3) came out of the sanctuary to the people.

This appearance, disappearance, and reappearance has its counterpart in our Great High Priest who will one day reappear "to those who are waiting for him" (Heb. 9:28). "V" Day is coming!

REVIEW

God's New Covenant is superior to the Old Covenant because of the:

I. *Person involved—God's Son (1:1—3:6)*
II. *Purpose intended—to provide redemption rest (3:7—4:13)*
III. *Priesthood interposed (4:14—8:5)*
IV. *Program inaugurated (8:6—10:18)*
 A. With a New Covenant (8:6—13)
 B. With a new sanctuary (9:1-10)
 C. With a better sacrifice (9:11—10:18)

The author will continue in Hebrews 10 contrasting the continual, imperfect, old sacrifices with Christ's perfect once-for-all offering.

CHAPTER
9
THE LET-US PATCH
Hebrews 10:1-39

Modern America has witnessed the mushrooming of in-'n'-out burger places, drive-in banks, drive-in laundries, etc. A person might almost get the picture of the Old Testament priesthood in Hebrews 10 by imagining a car driving in and out, in and out, in and out, around and around one of these modern drive-ins. As Hebrews depicts it, the Old Testament priesthood was virtually a walk-a-thon, a stand-a-thon. What they did, they "repeated endlessly" (Heb. 10:1).

Comedian Jack Benny used to have a character on his radio show dubbed the "floorwalker." Benny would get off the elevator in a department store and summon, "Oh, floorwalker." The person who played the part responded with an unforgettably funny "ye-e-es," almost as if in that one word he was trying to cover the entire musical scale. Old Testament priests were walkers—always on the go. Furthermore, they stood (10:11), never sat (1:3; 8:1) like our Great High Priest does.

We live in an era of "body language." The body language of the old priesthood broadcasted, "Never done." The posture of our Priest proclaims, "Done."

> Done is the work that saves,
> Once and forever done.
> —Horatius Bonar

Shadowville

The Old Testament set-up was, as it were, Shadowville, the wonderful miniature world of shadows (10:1). The New Testament realities have substance to them, and the Old Testament observances were shadowy outlines of better things ahead.

Donald Miller wrote, "I know a man who married rather late in life. One day, prior to his marriage, he saw a lovely portrait of a girl in the studio of an art professor. He asked the professor if he could take the portrait home and hang it on the wall. . . . The professor offered to introduce him to the girl. He demurred at that, for he . . . was afraid the living image would spoil the portrait. For four years that portrait hung on his wall. Finally, by accident he met the girl. It was love at first sight, and before long they were married."[1]

The danger for the readers of Hebrews was that of preferring the painting to the real person! God the Artist had been sketching rough, impressionistic pencilings for centuries in Old Testament characters (e.g., Moses, Deut. 18:15), events (e.g., the Exodus from Egypt—see Lk. 9:31, where "departure" translates the Greek word for "exodus"), and objects (the Word [Jesus] tabernacled [literally] among us, Jn. 1:14, thereby being the New Testament counterpart to the Old Testament tabernacle—the focal place where God met with humanity). But "in these last days" (Heb. 1:3) of the New Testament, God the Artist has drafted His final, full-orbed, full-color painting in the person of His own Son.

The priests' in-'n'out regimen should have served worshippers as a teaching technique. They should have paused to reason: What is God trying to convey to me through all of this nonstop activity?

The scientist Pavlov conditioned his dog to salivate by repetitious routine. He brought dog food and rang the bell so frequently that the dog's mouth was conditioned to expect food whenever the bell rang. In a sense God was ringing bells in the heads of the Israelites.

The endless, multitudinous, virtually nonstop reruns kept saying, "Sin, sin, sin, sin!" The overall broadcast of the Old Testament offerings said, "Sins are remembered" (10:3) rather than "Sins are removed."

? How is the remembrance of sins in Old Testament sacrifices (10:3) different from the remembrances in Christian Communion (I Cor. 11:24, 25)?

" The gospel transforms [remembrance] from a remembrance of guilt to a remembrance of grace!

—Philip Hughes, *Hebrews*

Jesus: God's Embodied Will

Since the author's mind is marinated in Old Testament Scripture, a Biblical light bulb lights up over his head as he talks (10:1, 3) about the inadequacy of Old Testament sacrifices. In Psalm 40:6-8 David expresses an amazing view of sacrifices.

Because the speaker in Psalm 40 says, "I have *come* . . . to do your will, O my God" (vs. 8), the author of Hebrews finds its chief fulfillment in the *Coming One* (a Messianic title for Christ, see Mt. 11:3; Jn. 6:14). Therefore, through the mouth of David proceeds the greater voice of David's son (Heb. 10:5). Listen. It is Christ who speaks in Psalm 40:6-8.

Notice that the author of Hebrews has changed

"my ears you have pierced" (Ps. 40:6)
to
"a body you prepared for me" (Heb. 10:5).

Most likely, we have here an example of a figure of speech called *synecdoche (suh-NECK-duh-key)*. This is where a writer uses a part for the whole of a thing. For instance, some Christian groups (see Acts 2:42) call Communion the breaking of bread. In that case, the bread (a part of the celebration) comes to stand for the whole (both bread and cup). Since the *ears* are the apparatus by which we intake commands and the *body* by which we carry out commands, the ears may be a synecdoche for the whole body. In execution of God's master will, a body was required for Jesus. Thus, the Incarnation—the enfleshment of Jesus. (Charles Wesley penned, "Veiled in flesh, the Godhead see, Hail the incarnate deity.") Jesus was the embodiment (literally) of the will of God. In a far greater sense than the lifelong Hebrew servant whose ears were pierced (Ex. 21:5, 6), Jesus' body was pierced (Ps. 22:16). "He was pierced for our transgressions" (Isa. 53:5).

The author of Hebrews says startlingly, that (in some sense) the Old Testament offerings were demanded by God, but not desired by Him (Heb. 10:8). God's "will" is referred to three times in 10:7-10. Jesus wanted to do what God wanted. "And by that will, we have been made holy through the sacrifice of the body of Jesus Christ once for all" (10:10).

The differences between the Old Testament priests and Christ the Priest can be charted:

Old Testament Priests (vs. 11)	*Our Priest (vs. 12)*
"day after day" "again and again"	"for all time"
"offers the same sacrifices"	"offered . . . one sacrifice"
"stands"	"sat down"

Ω "When sin is taken away, it is taken away from 'around' us. The [Greek] verb [for 'take away' in verse 11] is used in the middle voice in Gen. 41:42 (LXX) of Pharaoh 'taking off' his ring from around his finger. This makes us think of Tarzan muscularly unwinding the enveloping coils of some python from around its victim. Even so, the one who 'takes away' our sins can remove those enveloping coils from around us."[2] Like the new Christian who is also given new life, the risen Lazarus still had to have friends help unwind him from enveloping bands that hemmed him in.

? How can you help in delivering someone from some encircling sin-habit, as friends did for the linen-wrapped Lazarus? Has anyone helped you get delivered from some binding habit?

Just as we wait (9:28) for Christ to reappear, He "waits for his enemies to be made his footstool" (10:13). Verse 10 is resummarized in verse 14. Furthermore, part of his lengthy quote from Jeremiah 31:34 (in Heb. 8:8-12) is requoted in Hebrews 10:16, 17. The reason he requotes this item from Jeremiah is that it reinforces the author's argument and supplies his clincher. Unlike those sins that were re-remembered all during the Old Testament era, our sins are "remember[ed] no more" by God. Imagine—an omniscient God with amnesia!

In verse 18 the King James Version has the term "remission."

However, most people today think of remission of cancer (which generally means only a *temporary* release that will almost invariably recur). Therefore, "forgiven" is by far the better translation.

Being fully "forgiven" carries the corollary—"there is no longer any sacrifice for sin" (vs. 18). Imagine the thunderboltlike impact of these words on the person of Jewish descent during those turbulent years! In addition, Benjamin Warfield noted "wherever the Christian [missionary] religion went, there blood-sacrifice ceased to be offered—just as the tapers go out when the sun rises."[3]

Open Door Policy

At this juncture we need to pause. The reason is that almost all Bible scholars—if they divide Hebrews into only two parts—divide the book between

1:1—10:18
and
10:19—13:25

"Therefore" begins 10:19—and we should always ask: what is "therefore" there for? Here it acts as a hinge attaching the door of 10:19—13:25 to the wall of argument in 1:1—10:18.

Instead of an unrelenting consciousness about our sins (10:1-3), "we have confidence to enter the Most Holy Place" (10:19). The barking dog of conscience has been given a permanent muzzle.

The "open door policy" to God's presence is permitted "by a new and living way opened up for us through the curtain, that is, his body" (10:20). This curtain—the veil of the Jerusalem Temple—was anything but flimsy. It was probably about 60′ X 30′ and four or five inches thick when Jesus died. Matthew 27:51 informs us: "At that moment [that Jesus died] the curtain of the temple was torn in two from top to bottom."

The title of a series of high school Spanish textbooks was *El Camino Real* (the royal highway). Through His death, Jesus opened up *el camino real* to God.

The veil is rent: lo, Jesus stands
Before the throne of grace
And clouds of incense from his hands
Fill all that glorious place.

His precious blood is sprinkled there.
Before and on the throne
And his own wounds in heaven declare
The work that saves is done.
—James G. Deck

Since we have such a sacrifice (10:19, 20) and "since we have a great priest" (10:21)—both priestly sacrifice and sacrificing priest combined uniquely in one—there are certain deductions to draw. These deductions furnish us with the "let-us" patch of the Book of Hebrews:

> Let us draw near to God with a sincere heart in full assurance of faith, having our hearts sprinkled . . . and having our bodies washed . . . (vs. 22).
> Let us hold unswervingly . . . hope . . . (vs. 23).
> Let us . . . spur one another . . . toward love (vs. 24).
> Let us not give up meeting (vs. 25).

Warning Flare

From the Greek word for "spur" we get an English word "paroxysm." A "paroxysm" refers to a "fit" (whether literal convulsions or as in the expression "he threw a fit," i.e., temper tantrum). The Greek word is found only twice in the New Testament, the other reference being Acts 15:39, where Paul and Barnabas had a "sharp disagreement." Thus, we are to incite, stimulate, prod, exasperate one another (ha!)—to love.

After speaking (the only time in Hebrews) of "one another" (10:24), the author turns to the readers' collective togetherness in verse 25. Note here that this verse, so frequently used by pastors as a goad to church attendance, is usually used out of context. (Read verses 26, 27 along with 25 to see that this is not just church skipping. Very few would say, "Skip church and there's 'a fearful expectation of judgment and of raging fire' waiting for you!")

Verse 25 must be couched in the context of verses 26-31. The view taken here is that the author is alluding to apostasy (3:12)—a deliberate, defiant, defection from God. Perhaps a similar secession from church is referred to in I John 2:19 ("they went out").

A whole bundle of rods cannot be broken, though each rod in the bundle may be broken separately.

—Augustus Strong, *Systematic Theology*

COMPARISON

Hebrews 6:4-9	*Hebrews 10:26-32, 39*
"if they fall away" (vs. 6)	"if we deliberately keep on sinning" (vs. 26)
"tasted the goodness of the Word of God" (vs. 5)	"received the knowledge of the truth" (vs. 26)

"once been enlightened" (vs. 4)	"you had received the light" (vs. 32)
"shared in the Holy Spirit" (vs. 4)	"The Spirit of grace" (vs. 29)
"subjecting him [the Son of God] to public disgrace" (vs. 6)	"trampled the Son of God under foot" (vs. 29)
"dear friends, we are confident of better things in your case—things that accompany salvation" (vs.9)	"But we are not of those who shrink back and are destroyed, but of those who believe and are saved" (vs. 39)

CONTEXT

"We want . . . you to show . . . diligence to . . . inherit what has been promised" (vss. 11, 12)	"You need to persevere so that . . . you will receive what he [God] has promised" (vs. 36)

Hebrews 10:26-39 is one of the most devastating of the classic warning passages with which Hebrews is latticed (see also 2:1-4; 3:12-14; 4:11; 6:4-8; and 12:14-29). A number of scholars treat as substantially the same issue the subjects and passages charted below.

SUBSTANTIALLY THE SAME SUBJECT

The unpardonable sin	Mark 3:22-30
The second of the soil types in the Parable of the Four Soils.	Luke 8:13
Two who shipwrecked their faith	I Timothy 1:19, 20
One who "turns away from the living God"	Hebrews 3:12
Those who "fall away"	Hebrews 6:6

Those who "deliberately keep on sinning after [they] have received the knowledge of the truth."	Hebrews 10:26
Those who "have known the way of righteousness" and "turn[ed] their backs" on it.	II Peter 2:20-22
"Sin that leads to death" by "antichrists" who "went out from" the church.	I John 2:18, 19; 5:16

The backdrop for this deliberate sinning is the two-category breakdown for sins in Numbers 15:27-31 (see also Deut. 17:12 and Ezek. 18:26). In the second category is radical revolt from God, for which there was no sacrifice specified in the Old Testament. Indeed, the author argues from the lesser (the Old Testament situation) to the greater ("how much more severely") in verses 28 and 29.

Just as in Mark 3:22-30 the blasphemy against the Holy Spirit entails the contemptible repudiation of the Son of God, even so in Hebrews 10:29 there is a dual contempt shown for "the Son of God" and "the Spirit of grace." Apostates

"trampled the Son of God underfoot"
"insulted the Spirit of grace."

The Spirit of grace is referred to in Zechariah 12:10, and, interestingly, in that same context (12:3) the verb "trample" is used twice by the Septuagint (the Greek version of the Hebrew Old Testament) with reference to Jerusalem being trampled. Similarly, Zechariah 9:11 speaks of "the blood of my covenant with you," which may be reflected in the wording of Hebrews 10:29. Deuteronomy 32 (the farewell Song of Moses) is quoted twice (vs. 35 and 36) in Hebrews 10:30, reinforcing the ominous note of judgment (10:27-31).

The greatest deposit of detective clues (in Hebrews) for helping us make some positive identification of the book's original readers is clustered in Hebrews 10:32-34. The early Christian church leader Chrysostom said that the author acts here like a soul doctor, having first made a deep surgical incision and then applying soothing medication.[4] Criticism must be cushioned by comfort. Severe warnings need to be balanced with positive motivation.

Some of the detailed data we derive from verses 32-34 are:

1. public persecution in their past (vss. 32 and 33);
2. pity for those in prison (vs. 34); and
3. property confiscation (vs. 34).

? How do you think modern assertiveness books, such as *Winning Through Intimidation,* might handle issues like the one in Hebrews 10:34? Is all assertiveness wrong? (Check Acts 16:35-40 to answer.)

There is a built-in paradox in 10:34, making these readers' property confiscation emotionally manageable. They had realer (forgive the poor English!) estate elsewhere! And they had an emotional realization of that reality.

After a retrospective view (vss. 32-34) the author moves to a prospective view (vss. 35-39). Since

"He . . . will come" (vs. 37),
you "will be . . . rewarded" (vs. 35), and
"you will receive what he has promised" (vs. 36).

As in the earlier message of Hebrews 6:11 and 12, the author admonishes: persevere to what God has promised (10:36). This note of faith in the form of patient perseverance brings him a mental flashback to Habakkuk 2:3, 4.

Habakkuk: Heritage of Faith

Habakkuk 2:3, 4 is one of the truly monumental Old Testament texts, for it is used at three critical junctures in the New Testament (and one of them is the theme text for the book of Romans). "Romans [1:17] emphasizes the first two words [of Heb. 2:4], *the just*; Galatians [3:11] the second words, *shall live*; Hebrews [10:38] the last words, *by faith.*"[5]

In its context, Habakkuk is heralding the coming of the marauding and menacing Chaldeans (the neo-Babylonians). They are about to run over Judah like a bulldozer over an anthill. Habakkuk questions: how can a just God do this (use a less righteous people to punish a more righteous nation)? All the prophet can do is wait in f*wait*h (to coin a word). In light of the coming Chaldean conquerors, the ones who are right with God will simply go on living by faith.

"He who is coming" (the conquering Chaldean) becomes the Messiah (see Mt. 11:3) in Hebrews 10:37 (see 10:5 and 7).

This type of faith has a Sanforized quality about it (it doesn't shrink back; 10:38). Compare here Hebrews 6:4-8 plus 6:9 with 10:26-30 and 39.

6:4-8	*10:26-39*
Those (third person plural) who fall away *(6:6)*	"If we keep on deliberately sinning" *(10:26)*
Switch in personal pronoun . . . "*we* are persuaded . . . of *you* . . . things that accompany salvation" *(6:9)* (KJV)	switch in personal pronoun ("you" in 10:32, 36)—"*we* are not of *those* who shrink back . . . but . . . who believe and are saved" *(10:39)*

Since he has waved the banner of the classic *faith* text (Hab. 2:4), the author is now ready to launch into the honor roll of faith in Hebrews 11.

CHAPTER

10

WELCOME TO FAITHVILLE

Hebrews 11:1-40

Karl Marx said that religion was the opiate of the masses. In other words, the powerful could use faith in a "sweet bye-and-bye" to keep the poor masses from rising up for a better here and now. Was Marx right or wrong?

No doubt there is partial truth to Marx's claim. As a parallel, Bible quoters can use the command to "submit" in Ephesians 5:22 oppressively. Or, preachers who want to stay on a pedestal can preach sermons about how "God wants you to do the little thing He has given you to be faithful in," when in reality your contentment with "little" keeps you from infringing on such a pastor's protective territory. Yes, the notion of faith in the future can be misused to oppress people.

However, for the Christian, "what you see is what you get" is not the total truth. And for those who are exploited in this world (Heb. 10:34) there is "a better country—a heavenly one" (11:16) waiting where they will be rewarded (10:35, 36; 11:6). Meanwhile they must live "by faith"—that is the overarching theme of Hebrews 11. Eighteen sentences in this chapter begin with the refrain—"by faith." It has often been called the Honor Roll of Faith, or Faith's Hall of Fame. It is undoubtedly the most familiar chapter in Hebrews.

Verse 1 is not a formal, technical definition of faith, but an operational one in light of the context of the chapter. The NIV captures the parallelism: "Faith is being

> **sure**
> of what we hope for and
> **certain**
> of what we do not see."

Hebrews uses the word "faith" more than any other New Testament book. In this chapter it appears 24 times. Hebrews 11 is the amplified commentary upon Habakkuk 2:4 (see Heb. 10:37, 38).

Faith gives substance to what is shadowy, and solidity to what is not *seen.* "By faith we understand . . . that what is *seen* was not made out of what was visible" (vs. 3). Noah was warned "about things not yet *seen*" (vs. 7). The patriarchs only "*saw* [the promises] . . . from a distance" (vs. 13). By faith Moses "*saw* him who is invisible" (vs. 27).

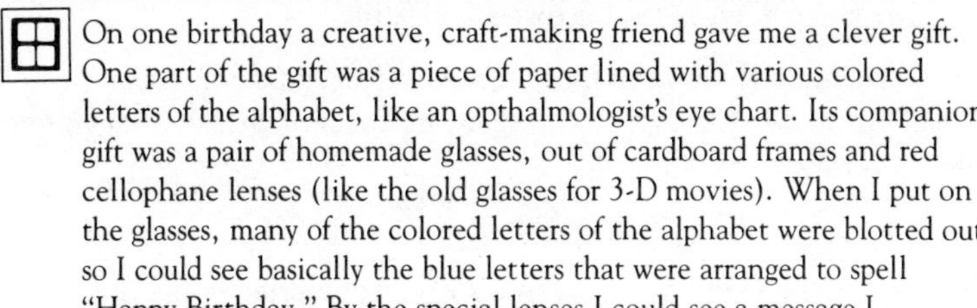
On one birthday a creative, craft-making friend gave me a clever gift. One part of the gift was a piece of paper lined with various colored letters of the alphabet, like an opthalmologist's eye chart. Its companion gift was a pair of homemade glasses, out of cardboard frames and red cellophane lenses (like the old glasses for 3-D movies). When I put on the glasses, many of the colored letters of the alphabet were blotted out so I could see basically the blue letters that were arranged to spell "Happy Birthday." By the special lenses I could see a message I ordinarily would not have seen. Faith provides us with lenses to the unseen.

The Jewish-Christian readership of Hebrews was having to face a crumbling world of the seen. A.D. 70 meant that the sensory world of burning sacrificial flesh, the tantalizing aroma of priestly incense, the multicolored wardrobe of priests, the gold and marble Temple was no longer available to their senses. They must now "live by faith, not by sight" (II Cor. 5:7).

Archaeologists have discovered papyri *(puh-PIE-ree)*—that is, ancient paperlike documents made from the pith of Nile River valley papyrus plants—in which the same Greek word translated "substance" in the King James Version of Hebrews 11:1 means "title deeds." Just as title deeds bring one into possession of property, so faith ushers one into the reality of the eternal unseen (II Cor. 4:18; 5:7).

Anaphora is the name of the literary style of a writer who repeats a word or phrase at the outset of at least several lines in a row for rhetorical effect. Hebrews 11 is one of the best examples of this technique found in any literature. Look at all the "by faith"s.

The miller's daughter in the fairy tale was forced to spin gold out of straw, but at least she had some raw material to start with! In the case of Creation we are forced to faith in the unseen at the outset, for "the universe was formed at God's command, so that what is seen was not made out of what was visible" (vs. 3). Halford Luccock told of the man who, upon first viewing the Grand Canyon, exclaimed, "My, something must have happened here!" Luccock went on to say it was plain that a farmer "did not drive a rude plow along the ground and thus create that vast chasm." How do we account for something so vast as the universe? Reason argues that the cause must be greater than the effect. Faith ratifies that this is so in the case of Creation.

Commentators have captured several valuable comparisons and contrasts in Hebrews 11:4-7. Simon Kistemaker[1] penned:

> "For his faith Abel paid the price of his life.
> Because of his faith Enoch was taken from this life.
> By faith Noah saved his own family's life."

Note that in all three cases faith became a life and death issue. "If in Abel faith speaks through a dead man, in Enoch it speaks through one who never died."[2]

Abel

Here is faith's en-ABEL-ment (chuckle!). Appropriately the first illustrious illustration in faith's honor roll is named Abel (we play deliberately on the same word sound as *able*). Actually, Cain was *able*, too (this is getting confusing, but God said so in Genesis 4:7—that he was *able* to please God if he acted appropriately).

Bible students debate why Abel's is labelled "a better sacrifice" (11:4) than Cain's. Was it because of the type of offerings, or the attitude of the offerers? The majority of Bible commentators believe (in keeping with the "by faith" theme of chapter 11) that the approvedness of the two characters lay not in the sacrifices *per se* but in the sacrificer's approach. It is true that sacrificial animals were acceptable at a later date in Mosaic history, but we have no explicitly recorded revelation in the early chapters of Genesis demanding blood sacrifice only. (Genesis 3:21 is an implied *description* of assumed sacrifice, but not a *prescription* to sacrifice.)

The famed Rembrandt has a painting with smoke from Abel's sacrifice ascending but none from Cain's, implying that God's imprimatur on the offerings came in the form of fire. While nothing so explicit is stated in Genesis, there are later Biblical cases where that happened (see Lev. 9:22-24; I Kings 18:38; and II Chron. 7:1). Because of Abel's acceptance, he was classified among those who are "righteous . . . by faith" (compare 10:38 with 11:4 where the same Greek words are used).

Enoch

It's a riddle: What is the only Bible translation (in fact, a translation by God Himself) within the Bible itself? The answer comes from the KJV of Hebrews 11:5—"Enoch was translated . . . because God had translated him."

Riddle #2: Who was the all-time winner at hide-and-seek? Answer: Enoch—"he could not be found" (11:5). Along with Elijah (II Ki. 2:11), Enoch was one of a duo of human beings who detoured right by death. (Enoch also held the distinction of being the father of earth's oldest man.)

The form of faith for Enoch was that he "pleased God." Since our author consistently used the Septuagint, he carried over this wording into his vignette of Enoch.

? Can you name some person you know, of whom you would say, "He (or she) pleases God"? How does this God-pleasingness make itself specifically apparent to you?

Since Enoch was "one who pleased God" (11:5), the author of Hebrews enlarged (in 11:6) upon just what is required "to please God." The *sine qua non* (or indispensable ingredient) for God-pleasingness is faith. At this juncture the author switches tracks from the noun ("faith") to its verb form ("believe") for the only time in all of this chapter on faith.

" Belief in God . . . cannot mean being persuaded of some entity, even a supreme entity.

—John A. T. Robinson, *Honest to God*

God is no longer a useful hypothesis. While a faint trace of God still broods over the world like the smile of a cosmic Cheshire cat, science and knowledge will soon rub that faint trace away.

—Julian Huxley

The author of Hebrews: "Anyone who comes to [God] must believe that he exists" (11:6).

Genuine faith hammocks itself upon two cardinal realities:

(1) the actual God—"believe that he exists," and

(2) the acting God—"that he rewards these who earnestly seek him." This is no deistic, do-nothing deity who once upon a time wound up the world clock and has now retired to twiddle His thumbs!

To "believe" God means to "seek him" (11:6). An active God requires active faith. Faith works.

Since the "righteous . . . will live by faith" (10:38), Noah "became heir of the righteousness that comes by faith" (11:7). Since "faith is being . . . certain of what we do not see" (11:1), Noah acted "by faith . . . when warned about things not yet seen" (11:7). "By his faith he condemned the world" (11:7) as "a preacher of righteousness" (II Pet. 2:5) as "the outward call echoed from every hammer blow that was struck in building the ark."[3]

Abraham (8-19)

The verses concentrating on Abraham can be outlined as follows:
(1) faith perceives a place (8-10);
(2) faith conceives a posterity (11-16);
(3) faith receives a promise (17-19).

First, heroic faith steps out in an adventure (8-10). John Henry Jowett proclaimed, "Merely to hug a creed and to take no risk is no more faith than to hug a timetable is to take a journey."[4] C. S. Lewis spoke of his many-stopovered journey to Christ as a "spiritual safari." Warren Wiersbe said that *Abraham left no forwarding address.*[5]

Not only did Abraham not know where he was heading when he left Chaldea (vs. 8), he never had perma-property stakes when he got to Canaan (vs. 9). "Abraham's stay in Canaan was as temporary as the pegs he drove into the ground to keep his tents pitched."[6] Abraham was the original Philip Nolan—a "man without a country."

Secondly, heroic faith specializes in impossibilites (11-16). Humanly speaking, Isaac was an impossibility, but "without faith it is impossible to please God" (11:6). Sarah's womb was a tomb (Rom. 4:19), but Abraham believed "the God who gives life to the dead and calls things that are not as though they were" (Rom. 4:17). In modern times there have been Jews like Sigmund Freud, Albert Einstein, Jonas Salk, and multitudes more of such world changers because Abraham's faith was in the God who was faithful (Heb. 11:11). As Abraham scanned "the stars in the sky and . . . sand on the seashore" (11:12), he became an "imagineer" of faith, believing that God could produce a posterity that prolific from a couple of senior citizens.

Thirdly, heroic faith sacrifices its dearest possessions (17-19). Trust has its tests. In Abraham faith faced the classic contradiction: God had informed Abraham that Isaac was to be the means of this multiplication, yet God also told him to "sacrifice his one and only son" (11:17).

Have you ever wrestled with a situation where your attempt to obey God seemed to bring you into contradiction with what God had said in Scripture?

Faith, mighty faith, the promise sees
　　And looks to God alone;
Laughs at impossibilities,
　　And cries, "It shall be done."

Isaac and Jacob (20-21)

"By faith Isaac *blessed* Jacob" (11:20).
"By faith Jacob . . . *blessed* . . . Joseph's sons" (11:21).

The faith of father and son faced futureward. It is not enough to remember the "good old days" nostalgically. Frequently Biblical faith has to focus on the future even when only bleakness is broadcast on the horizon (eg., Hab. 3:17-19).

Joseph (22)

Like father—and grandfather, like son. Joseph saw that "his end" (11:22) was not the end. We have the expression "he felt it in his bones," but Joseph had faith, with reference to his bones, by living with escalated expectancy.

Moses (23-27)

First, notice the perspective of his parents (vs. 23). As the author of Ecclesiastes (3:1-8) *might* say, "there is a time to hide." Paul hid on one occasion (Acts 9:23-25). Usually we think of hiding as cowardly, yet "by faith" both Moses' parents (11:23) and Moses (11:27; Ex. 2:15) engaged in hiding.

Can you think of a modern instance where running and hiding might be an act of faith?

Second, note the choice of persecution instead of pleasure (vss. 24-27). In an age of pleasure mongers, Moses might be counseled by a psychiatrist to loosen up. After all, Moses "refused" (24), he "chose to be mistreated" (24), "he regarded disgrace . . . as of . . . value" (26).

Is this guy a masochist (i.e., one who takes pleasure in being abused)? Psychologists tell us that we prefer *homeostatic* environments—that is, we want everything to run smoothly in our personal lives. That is what makes Moses a faith figure here. By faith he moved beyond personal conveniences and comforts to hook up with a bunch of "losers."

How might a Christian today validly make some nonpleasurable choices like Moses did?

Moses made the tough choice to forego "the pleasures of sin for a short time." Like refined sugar, salty potato chips, chocolate candy, and much junk food, there is sin that is pleasurable, but the net result of enjoying it is long-term disaster.

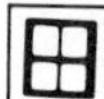
Ulysses and his sailors were returning from adventures in the Trojan War. They had been warned, by Circe, of the Siren singers of the Mediterranean—who would sing so sweetly, but eventually lure the sailors to their doom. Circe said that Ulysses should stop up his men's ears with wax and have them tie him to the mast. However, they did not need to resort to such measures because aboard ship was Orpheus, an even sweeter singer than the Sirens.[7]

Just as the sailors were not lured away to doom by the pleasurable Sirens, even so Moses was not lured away by "the pleasures of sin" in Egypt because he possessed something "of greater value than the treasures of Egypt" (11:26).

What kept Moses going? Moses "persevered because he saw him who is invisible" (11:27). He saw the unseen.

Some men see things as they are and say "Why?" I dream things that are not and say, "Why not?" —Robert F. Kennedy

He [God] can remove the cataract from the eye of faith.
—F. E. Marsh, *The Spiritual Life*

The Passing Over and the Passing Through (28, 29)

All the Israelite firstborn were saved by the Passover. All the Israelites were saved by the passing through of the Red Sea. Contrastingly, the saving of the Israelites meant the perishing of the Egyptians. As one homespun preacher put it, "God clabbered the Red Sea and clobbered the Egyptians."

Joshua and Rahab (30, 31)

Just as verse 29 recounted an event in which some were saved while others perished, so also verses 30 and 31 tell of an incident of simultaneous salvation and destruction—Jericho perished while Rahab was spared.

The Feats and 'Defeats' of Faith (32-40)

A noble army, men and boys,
The matron and the maid,
Around the Savior's throne rejoice,
In robes of light arrayed;
They climbed the steep ascent of heaven
Through peril, toil, and pain;
Oh God, to us may grace be given
To follow in their train.
—Reginald Heber

Hebrews 11:32-40 contains a collage of anonymous folks who "climbed the steep ascent of heaven through peril, toil, and pain." This type of persecution is not unique to Christianity. One Russian historian wrote of Jews persecuted by Russian Cossacks from 1648-'58: "Killing was accompanied by barbarous tortures; the victims were flayed alive, split asunder, clubbed to death, roasted on coals, or scalded with boilng water. Thousands of Jewish infants were thrown into wells, or buried alive."[8]

? What do you discover by comparing Hebrews 11:32-35a with 11:35b-38? What lesson can you learn from this?

After naming four judges, one king, and one prophet in verse 32 (but not in their chronological order), the author enlarges his faith roster to include many more miscellaneous forms of faith (33-38). By comparing verses 32-35a with 35b-38 we learn an interesting lesson—there are both feats and "defeats" of faith, both exploits and the exploited by faith.

Faith does not freeze into a single form. There is no Xeroxed faith. Some experienced mighty miracles by faith (32-35a). Others were "losers" by faith (35b-38). In some cases "women received back their dead, raised [miraculously] to life again" (35a), whereas others by faith died to "gain a better resurrection" (35b).

The problem is that we (including Christians) tend to applaud the "winners"-by-faith (who "escaped the edge of the sword," vs. 34), but overlook or look down on the "losers"-by-faith (such as those who "were put to death by the sword," vs. 37). Haddon Robinson said, "The writer of Hebrews offers us something desperately needed—a theology for losers! The right to fail is one of the few freedom's that our society does not allow its citizens. [How many Christian college alumnus publications print reports such as, "Stuart in California lost his wife and business last year, but he's still going on for God."]

Robinson continues: "When was the last time your church heard the testimony of a fink? Many youth rallies feature the athlete who scored the winning touchdown and gives credit to God. How about a word from the chap who fumbled the ball and by the grace of God managed to keep on going?

"The Bible does not urge us to go out and lose for the sheer therapy of losing or to fail because failing is more spiritual. The same faith that enables them [in Hebrews] to do exploits enables them to endure reverses." Paul could say—whether poverty or prosperity—"I can do everything through" Christ (Phil. 4:13—noting that the "everything" includes being "in need" in 4:12). Whereas the apostle James in Acts 12 was killed by the sword (2), the apostle Peter (in the same chapter) was delivered from the sword—both "by faith."

Most Bible scholars hold that Hebrews 11:34-38 probably refers to the heroes of the Maccabean era.

In the tapestry of time the hand of God weaves as many somber skeins as bright-hued silks.

—John Briggs, in *The Eerdmans Handbook of the History of Christianity*

Of the species of faith-folk sketched out in verses 32-38, the author of Hebrews paid the compliment, "The world was not worthy of them" (38). Some people these days treat animals better than they do humans. In fact, there is a Bide-a-Wee Association's Pet Memorial Park [an animal cemetery] on Long Island, New York, where there are 65,000 animals buried, including a grasshopper named Gary.[9] Some people pay huge sums to bury animals, but Hebrews recounts believers who were treated like earth's offscouring and refuse. By contrast, God's evaluation is: "the world was not worthy of them" (vs. 38).

C. T. Studd, missionary to three different countries, told the following story:

At the end of an address on the text, "He is able to save to the uttermost" [said C. T.] after the congregation had left, a single Chinaman remained behind, right at the back of the room. When we went to him, he told us we had been talking sheer nonsense. He said, "I am a murderer, an adulterer, I have broken all the laws of God and man again and again. I am also a confirmed opium smoker. He cannot save me." We laid before him the wonders of Jesus and His Gospel and His power. The man meant business, and was soundly converted. He said, "I must go to the town where I have done all this evil and sin, and in

> that very place tell the good tidings." He did. He gathered crowds, was brought before the mandarin, and was ordered 2,000 strokes with the bamboo, till his back was one mass of red jelly, and he himself was thought to be dead. He was brought back by some friends, taken to the hospital and nursed by Christian hands, till he was, at last, able to sit up. He then said, "I must go back . . . and preach this Gospel." We strongly dissuaded him, but a short time after he escaped and started preaching in the same place. Once more he was brought before the court. They were ashamed to give him the bamboo again, so sent him to prison. But the prison had small open windows and holes in the wall. Crowds collected, and he preached out of the windows and holes till, finding he did more preaching inside the prison than out, they set him free, in despair of ever being able to move one so stubborn and so staunch. Such men are ***worth*** saving.[10]

Along with those Old Testament worthies of chapter 11 and those believers of whom "the world was not worthy" (11:38) are the countless who are "worth saving." These worthies all bow before His Worthship, the One (in 12:1-3) who is worthy of our worship.

CHAPTER

11

STEADY IN A SHAKY SITUATION

Hebrews 12:1-29

F. B. Meyer penned, "When, in his Egyptian campaign, the Emperor Napoleon was leading his troops through the neighborhood of the Pyramids, he . . . said, 'Soldiers, forty centuries look down on you.' "[1] Those initial readers of Hebrews 11 had several centuries of the figures of faith looking down on them.

The first readers were "surrounded by such a great cloud of witnesses" (12:1). Again, F. B. Meyer enables us to visualize:

> *In some of the more spacious amphitheaters of olden times, the spectators rose in tier above tier to the number of 40 or 50,000; and to the . . . combatant as he looked around on this vast multitude of . . . faces, set in varied and gorgeous coloring, these vast congregations must have appeared like clouds, composed of infinitesimal units, but all making up one mighty aggregate, and bathed in such lines as are cast on the clouds at sunrise or sunset by the level sun.*[2]

Christian Olympics (12:1-3)

Thus, we are transported in our mind's eye to the athletic arena, where we are summoned to "run . . . the race marked out for us" (12:1). This is not a 100-yard dash, but an endurance race. Therefore, we are to:

1. "consider him [Christ] who endured" (12:3); and
2. "endure hardship as discipline" (12:7).

In verses 1-13 Christians are viewed as:

1. distance runners (1, 2);
2. disciplined children (4-11);
3. decision-making adults (12, 13).

First, the Christian runner has *fans*—spectators seated in the stands. In a stadium a runner sees the spectators not as individuals but as a single blurred mass—a cloud. The early Greek bard Homer referred to "a cloud of foot soldiers," using the same metaphor. The Old Testament stands (Heb. 11) are, as it were, filled with former gold-medal runners, whose examples urge us on.

Secondly, the Christian runner must enjoy a *freedom*. The author urges us to "throw off everything that hinders and the sin that so easily entangles" (12:1).

D. L. Moody once walked onto the preaching platform wearing a large backpack strapped on his shoulders. He informed the listeners that his backpack contained no whiskey bottle, or dice, or anything they might consider sinful in itself. He then asked his audience if they thought he could speak for Christ like that. Moody made his point: *even harmless things that hinder are harmful.*

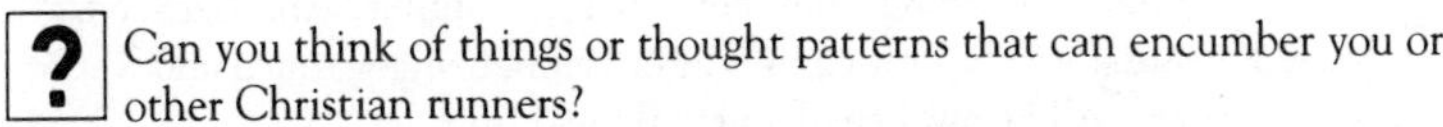

Can you think of things or thought patterns that can encumber you or other Christian runners?

When Grant started out to capture Vicksburg, he took nothing with him but a gun coat and a toothpick.

—a Civil War historian

The besetting weakness of middle age is self-complacency and unadventurous acceptance of things as they are.

—Bishop Stephen Neill, in Paul Rees, *Triumphant in Trouble*

Not only must we "throw off everything that hinders," but also "the sin that so easily entangles" (12:1). The verb form used here can have the sense of "encircling." It reminds one "of the ring of wild beasts in the jungle that encircle the camp-fire at night, each ready to pounce upon a careless victim."[3]

Thirdly, the Christian runner must run with *fortitude*, i.e., endurance or "perseverance" (12:1). David Hubbard likened the situation to the anchor runner in a relay race, heading toward the tape at the finish line. Above all else, he must not drop the baton. If we may extend this idea, the Old Testament runners (in chap. 11) are the others on the relay team who have handed the baton on to us. Now we must run the cinder track with perseverance.

Fourthly, The Christian runner must maintain his *focus*—"let us fix our eyes on Jesus" (12:2), the Eternal Miler. He is our gold-medal model (12:2, 3).

Those Old Testament believers apart from us could not "be made perfect" (11:40), for Jesus is the "perfecter of our faith" (12:2). As someone has said, we must:

Keep our mind on the exemplars,
Keep our legs on the go,
Keep our feet on the track,
Keep our body unweighted, and
Keep our eyes on Jesus.

Divine Discipline (12:4-13)

Now author functions like a railroad switchman. He switches tracks from his racing illustration to the home front. From Jesus as Champion Runner we now move to God as Disciplinarian in 12:4-11.

Any context in which you can be thoroughly comfortable is likely to prove deadening. A seed wrapped in sterilized cotton and sheltered in a vault may lie there a long time, but it will not sprout. Another seed, tossed where it will be chilled by winter before being warmed and wet by spring rains, will be awakened and will yield fruit.

—Webb Garrison, *Creative Imagination in Preaching*

The author of Hebrews takes his jumping-off point from Proverbs 3:11, 12 (in Heb. 13:5, 6). Some form of the term "discipline" appears ten times in Hebrews 12:5-11. Just as no mother would run up to someone else's naughty child in a supermarket and begin spanking her, so divine discipline denotes spiritual sonship. God corrects His own children. Correction is not condemnation. The judge who may have that same day sentenced young offenders to delinquency centers will not do the same thing if he returns home to find his own son has stolen money from family sources. "He does not put on his judicial robes and call court into session."[4]

In fact, correction is an earmark of care. The parent who cares corrects. This has been borne out by a three-year research project by Norman and Harris in conjunction with Xerox Education Publications and Crossley Surveys, Inc. One hundred sixty thousand teenagers were surveyed. The surveyors concluded from their research that teenagers want to be disciplined because they equate discipline with love.[5]

The author of Hebrews indicates that the adversities and aggravations we encounter are forms of divine discipline (12:7). He argues from the lesser (our human parents) to the greater (the Heavenly Parent) in 12:9, 10, though there are discernible differences.

Discipline is painful rather than pleasant. However, sometimes tragedy and adversity are the only ways God can get our attention.

God whispers to us in our pleasures, speaks in our conscience, but shouts in our pains: it is His megaphone to rouse a deaf world.

—C. S. Lewis, *The Problem of Pain*

A schoolmaster, Dr. Allan Heely, was once asked by someone the ideal curriculum for growing boys. He replied, "Any program of worthwhile studies so long as all of it is hard and some of it is unpleasant." —Quoted in Frank Gaebelein, *Varied Harvest*

Can you recall an experience when something previously painful later produced something more pleasant?

Perhaps our author returns to his athletic theme in referring to "those who have been trained" by this discipline (12:11). In verses 12 and 13 there are two items any runner must consider—the condition of his physique (12:12) and the condition of the path (12:13) on which he is running. Jay Adams comments on verse 12: "The relaxed arms and feeble knees . . . represent a condition impossible for participation in sports. His [an athlete's] muscle tone must be honed to a fine edge." And on verse 13's "level paths" (Prov. 4:26) Adams comments, "A man with a bad foot who walks among potholes is likely to do himself more harm."[6]

Two Wrong Responses (12:14-17)

In the gripping story *Most Deadly Game* a man on an island finds that he is the hunted prey stalked by an insane hunter. Similar picture language works its way into Hebrews 12:14. A. T. Robertson captures the flavor of it by paraphrasing, "Give peace a chase as if in a hunt."[7] Psalm 34:14 urges us to pursue peace. Peace (in 12:11) is a product of responding rightly to God's discipline.

To a Hebrew mind, peace carried overtones of wellness (being a rough equivalent to our street greeting, "How are you?"), integratedness, wholeness. Wholeness is assuredly related to holiness. F. B. Meyer explains the statement, "Without holiness no one will see the Lord," as follows: "A room or public building may be full of delicious sunlight. But that sunlight is not the [inherent] property of the room. You cannot congratulate it upon its possession. So the human spirit has no holiness apart from God."

Peace and holiness are two right paths to pursue. However, the author makes it clear in verses 15-17 that it is possible to respond wrongly. Two wrong responses are:

1. bitterness (15 cf. Deut. 29:18);
2. callousness (16, 17).

? How can you illustrate bitterness cropping up in your experience or circle of acquaintances? How can it be nipped in the bud or dealt with responsibly?

Damon Runyon, prince of New York columnists, died of tongue cancer. He stated, "The toughest thing for the victim to overcome is the feeling of resentment that it should have happened to him. 'Why me?' he keeps asking himself . . . . 'Of all the millions of people around, why me?' "[8]

In 1967, a 40-year-old school board member, churchgoer, Boy Scout leader, and father, named Leo Held, lived in Lock Haven, Pennsylvania. There were certainly some tip-offs to his troubled condition, but nobody expected him to walk into the paper mill where he'd worked and unleash a volley of 30 shots. He'd had a few prior feuds, including lack of job promotions and hitting a 71-year-old widow with a branch in a spat. Finally, a posse wounded Held after his shooting orgy. Under the picture of the wounded marksman *Time* magazine[9] ran the caption—"Responsible, respectable—and resentful."

If, on the one hand, there is the danger of poisonous resentment, on the other hand there is the risk of unresponsive indifference (12:16, 17), as exemplified in Esau, who bartered away the blessing of his birthright. Unlike Moses, Esau would rather "enjoy . . . pleasures . . . for a short time" (11:25). A growling stomach got the best of him (Gen. 25:29-34).

? Can you share a time when you blew an opportunity because you were unwilling to wait?

Last Warning (12:18-29)

Desert motorists may see the sign: "Last chance for gas. Next station 50 miles." Hebrews 12:18-29 contains the climactic, final warning bell of the book. Since the author has just mentioned "see[ing] the Lord" (12:14), he proceeds to paint that scene with resplendent wonder. Here is a most vivid display of realized eschatology—the future world bursts into the present.

On his deathbed, Puritan Richard Baxter exclaimed concerning our passage: "That Scripture is worth a thousand, thousand thoughts."[10]

In Harriet Beecher Stowe's classic *Uncle Tom's Cabin*, little Eva sat beside the dying slave, Uncle Tom. She read to him the section before us. His soul drank in the words eagerly. If God could integrate Heaven with a slave into such an august body, how could humans set the same person on an auction block for sale?

Notice the parallel structure in the section:

"You have not come to a mountain [Sinai]," (12:18)

but

"you have come to Mount Zion . . ." (12:22).

We must close our eyes and envision the scene at Sinai in Hebrews 12:18-21. It is ominous, foreboding, charged with overtones of fear. God's sound effects operated. The props outdid MGM Grand. It was God's dazzling fireworks display. Exodus 19:18, 19 sketches it.

The terrors of law and of God
    With me can have nothing to do;
My Savior's obedience and blood
    Hide all my transgressions from view.
        —Augustus Toplady

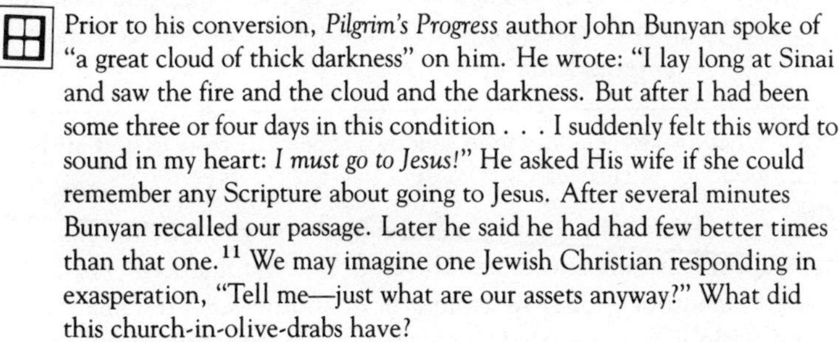

Prior to his conversion, *Pilgrim's Progress* author John Bunyan spoke of "a great cloud of thick darkness" on him. He wrote: "I lay long at Sinai and saw the fire and the cloud and the darkness. But after I had been some three or four days in this condition . . . I suddenly felt this word to sound in my heart: *I must go to Jesus!*" He asked His wife if she could remember any Scripture about going to Jesus. After several minutes Bunyan recalled our passage. Later he said he had had few better times than that one.[11] We may imagine one Jewish Christian responding in exasperation, "Tell me—just what are our assets anyway?" What did this church-in-olive-drabs have?

F. B. Meyer summarizes it: "To how great splendor had these Hebrew Christians been accustomed—marble courts, throngs of white-robed Levites, splendid vestments, the . . . pomp of symbol, ceremonial and choral psalm!

"And to what a contrast they were reduced—a meeting in some hall or school, with the poor, afflicted and persecuted members of a despised and hated sect."[12]

? Have you ever felt like you or someone you know has had to give up a lot in the cause of Christ?

Hebrews 12:22-24 marches out on to the parade ground the assets Christians have. The Greek verb "you have come" is the one from which we get our English word "proselyte," thereby signalling the readers' conversion. Also notice that for every item those Jewish believers had to give up, they gained immeasurably in spiritual trade-offs.

Parading out the lineup, the author asserted that his readers had come:

1. "to thousands upon thousands of angels . . .";
2. "to the church of the firstborn";
3. "to God, the judge of all . . .";
4. "to the spirits of righteous men made perfect";
5. "to Jesus the mediator of a New Covenant,"; and
6. "to the sprinkled blood" of Christ.

Here is indeed a lineup of sluggers—of Babe Ruths and Lou Gehrigs, spiritually speaking.

The Amplified Version refers to "the countless multitudes of angels in festal gathering" (12:22). One is reminded by its festive atmosphere of stingy Ebenezer Scrooge, in Dickens's *A Christmas Carol*, thinking back to the gala Christmas parties thrown by his boss, Mr. Fezziwig, when he was a young man. The festiveness of a Fezziwig Christmas party, a Cratchitt family Christmas dinner, or the "music and dancing" (Lk. 15:25) upon the prodigal son's return foreshadow the celebration of the heavenly Jerusalem.

? What joyous memories from your own experience seem to hint at the future joy of Heaven?

Instead of reminding us of Esau, the firstborn who forfeited his heirship, the author showcases "the church of the firstborn" (12:23). Then, the author explicitly reminds us of another Old Testament character in verse 24—Abel. Abel's life was taken involuntarily, but Christ's life was given voluntarily.

God certainly has His attention-getting devices—what a sound system verses 25-28 reveal! If Sinai shook (vs. 26), what will it be like (according to Haggai 2:6) to undergo a heavenquake? Yet God has a purpose in all this shaking—as if He were wielding the elements in a giant sifter—"so that what cannot be shaken may remain" (12:27). The original readers must have felt as if they were caught in an automatic blender or trapped in a laundromat dryer. Their emotional world had the shakes. However, sometimes a shake-up causes us to discover what is really nailed down. In a world coming unglued, we have "a kingdom that cannot be shaken" (12:28). "Not a fragment of heaven's masonry shall crumble beneath the shock."[13]

The mixture which is not shaken decomposes.

—Heraclitus

CHAPTER

12

SCATTERSHOT ADVICE

Hebrews 13 / Review

Dot-dot-dash. Dash-dot-dash-dash. That's something like the rhythmic pattern of Hebrews 13—literary Morse code. The reason for this scattershot effect is because there are some 20 commands on 15 different topics in Hebrews 13.

That does not mean that we are faced with a logicless letter ending to Hebrews. He starts with the social sphere:

Verse 1: brothers;
Verse 2: strangers;
Verse 3: prisoners.

The author, probably having a flashback to Genesis 18, asserts that hospitality could conceivably result in one's entertaining angels (13:2).

⊞ One might expect some glazed-eyed character from a city park in downtown Los Angeles to claim to have had angel visitors, but how about a president of Wheaton College (a Christian college in Illinois)? Wheaton president V. Raymond Edman had been a missionary in South America. He was living on a fairly remote missionary compound. During one particular season of discouragement, Edman was visited by an older person he had never seen before. Their conversation was tremendously helpful to the discouraged missionary. After the visitor left, Edman jumped up to go out and thank the visitor. He ran out to the gate which was the only way in and out of the compound. A guard had been sitting there, and Edman asked where the stranger was who had just left. The mystified gate guard responded that there had been no one in or out of the gate for hours. Edman had to conclude finally that he had been the recipient of the blessing of Hebrews 13:2—that he was one of those who had "entertained angels without knowing it."

There is a buttonhook in logic between verses 2 and 3. After the readers have been exhorted to have travelers into their homes, they are then exhorted to leave their homes to visit prisoners sympathetically.[1] (If you wish to implement the first exhortation more often, you may wish to purchase Marlene LeFever's book *Creative Hospitality* for ideas on how to go about it.)

From relationships outside the home (13:1-3), the author shifts to the key relationship in the home—marriage (13:4). If Hebrews 13:4 treats the commandment, "You shall not commit adultery" (Ex. 20:14), verse 5 reflects two other of the Ten Commandments ("You shall not steal . . . not covet," Ex. 20:15, 17).

" SEX: SUB-CHRISTIAN VIEWS IN CHURCH HISTORY

Some of the church fathers goofed. Irenaeus (about 180 A.D.) reported that Gnostics believed "that marriage and procreation are from Satan."[2] Marcion (another heretic in the second century) spoke of the "disgusting paraphernalia of reproduction."[3] Augustine (a great church leader about A.D. 300) wrote that "the gateway to hell lay between a woman's thighs."[4] Jerome (another great church leader about A.D. 300) spoke of "the bestial act of intercourse."[5] He also said, "Anyone who is too passionate a lover with his own wife is himself an adulterer."[6] Peter Lombard (theologian about A.D. 1100) warned "that the Holy Spirit left the room when a married couple had relations, even if for the purpose of conceiving a child."[7]

Fortunately, Martin Luther (about A.D. 1540) held a healthier view—that "the marital embrace might be a good posture in which to be found when Jesus returns."[8] Cornelius Plantinga, Jr., said, in line with Hebrews 13:4—"Sex for Christians . . . is a joy . . . not a toy. You do not play with fire. Sex needs a context. It needs a fireplace."[9]

Just as there can be dangerous desires for intimacy outside of marriage (13:4), even so there can be dangerous desires for more and more money (13:5). Quotes adapted from Deuteronomy 31:6 (in Heb. 13:5) and Psalm 118:6, 7 (in Heb. 13:6) reinforce the author's assertion.

Having dealt with social involvements in 13:1-6, the author turns to spiritual ideas in 13:7-17, taking the form of leaders and their teachings. The word in the past tense in 13:7 ("spoke") zeroes in on their past Christian leaders who had passed off the scene, whereas the present verb tenses in verses 17 and 24 focus on their present leadership. Leaders change, but Christ never changes (13:8). He is the contemporary of all the centuries.

I change, He changes not;
The Christ can never die.
His love, not mine, the resting place;
His truth, not mine the tie.
—Horatius Bonar

Hebrews 13:8, so frequently seen gracing wall plaques, in its context refers to "the outcome of their [i.e., the leaders'] way of life." For humans, nothing is so changeless as change. Yet, in the midst of life's air pockets and bumps, we can find solidity in the never-changing Christ.

Because we are anchored to the essential and eternal Christ (13:8), we should not be overly occupied with the out-of-the-ordinary ("strange teachings," 13:9) or the outward ("ceremonial foods," 13:9).

Ω Bizarre teachings are available in every shade. If we would give the Greek word for "strange" (13:9) a woodenly literal rendering, it would be something like "many colored." The same word is used of the rainbow variety of temptations in James 1:2 ("many kinds") that beseige us. The strange doctrines that arrive in canary yellow or flaming flamingo are not too difficult to detect, but watch out for the ones that approach in shades of pastel!

Philip Hughes summarized Hebrews 13:9—"Food goes into the stomach for the strengthening of the body; but only grace strengthens the heart."[10] "Ceremonial foods" (13:9) would be associated with Jewish altars. Reading between the lines, we must assume that some antagonists were claiming (like children with their "nyah, nyahs"), "We have an altar" (13:10). Shockingly, the Christian altar is one from which traditional priests are disqualified.

"Outside the camp" (13:11, 13) and "outside the city gate" (13:12) would be where the Jews' garbage dump was located. Jesus died, as it were, on unholy ground (Jn. 19:20). Compare Leviticus 4:12; 6:9-11; 13:46; 24:23; Numbers 5:3; 15:35, 36, and 19:3.

James Russell Lowell wrote:

"New occasions teach new duties;
Time makes ancient good uncouth:
They must upward still and onward
Who would keep abreast of truth."

"Let us, then, go to him outside the camp, bearing the disgrace he [Jesus] bore" (13:13). We need "grace" (13:9) to face such "disgrace" (13:13). Note how much Hebrews 13:9-16 is riddled with Old Testament terminology.

> **?** What words do you spot in Hebrews 13:9-16 that are flavored with an Old Testament overtone?

The Christian's "sacrifices" are what we say (13:15) and "do" (13:16). "Good" unscrambled, becomes "go do"! To "do good" is to go do. We praise God and we practice goodness.

Not only should we remember past leaders' legacies (13:7), but we should also obey current leaders (13:17). Like those familiar shepherds of the Christmas scene "keeping watch over their flocks" (Lk. 2:8), faithful pasturers (i.e., pastors and leaders) "watch over you" (Heb. 13:17). The New English Bible renders it: "They are tireless in their concern for you."

As a kind of remote-control leader, the author requests prayer for himself (Heb. 13:18, 19) before he prays for his readers (13:20, 21). Simon Kistemaker pointed out how sparingly the author has used the pronoun "I" up to this point (only twice in 11:32), but now the personal "I" irrupts in 13:19.[11]

George Turner acclaimed the benedictory prayer of 13:20 and 21 "the greatest in all the Scriptures."[12] Interestingly, only here in all of this piece written to the Hebrews is the resurrection of Christ mentioned explicitly. (Of course, it is assumed every time the ascended Christ is mentioned, as in 1:3 and 8:1. If Christ rose up to Heaven, He had to rise up from the tomb.)

Not only had the Hebrews had model shepherds (or leaders, 13:7, 17, 24), but they had "that great Shepherd of the sheep" (13:20). Hence, to impel them "to do good" (13:16), that Shepherd would "equip [them] with everything *good* for *do*ing his will" (13:21). With that equipment Christian pilgrims surely ought to make progress.

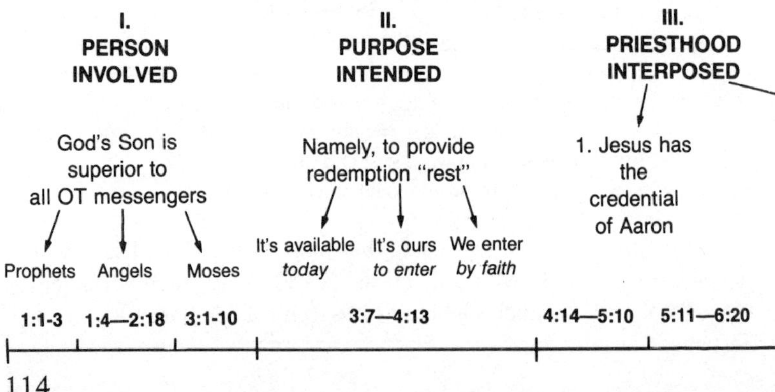

At the conclusion of Hebrews (13:22-24) there are three tantalizing tidbits that furnish us with hints about: (1) The texture of the writing (13:22); (2) a friend of the writer (13:23); and (3) the place of writing (13:24). Unfortunately, however, the three are still enshrouded in misty obscurity.

First, because the writing is labeled both "a word of exhortation" (a term used for Paul's sermon in Acts 13:15) and "a short letter" (Heb. 13:22), we have called it a homiletter (a coined word, denoting the hybrid of a sermon—or homily—in the form of a letter).

Secondly, we are given a tip-off about Timothy (13:23). It is assumed that the expression "has been released" presumes some prison term. However, the New Testament nowhere else tells of an imprisonment of Timothy. Furthermore, Hebrews 13:23 is the last we hear of Timothy in the New Testament.

Just as there is obscurity about the reference to Timothy's imprisonment (13:23), there is even greater ambiguity about the expression "Those from Italy" (13:24). Does it mean:

> I, the writer, am in Italy, and Christian folks here with me send you greetings;
>
> or
>
> I, the writer, am far removed from Italy, and as I write back to Italy, "Those [once hailing] from Italy" here with me pass on their greetings.

It would appear that the author of Hebrews was writing *to* or *from* Italy, but which of these is true is not absolutely transparent.

Although the majority of orthodox scholars agree that it is unlikely that Paul authored this homiletter, the mystery writer of Hebrews closes with the trademark of Paul—the term "grace" (13:25). Grace is the quintessence of the Gospel. "Grace be with you all." Now let's get the synthesized sweep of Hebrews.

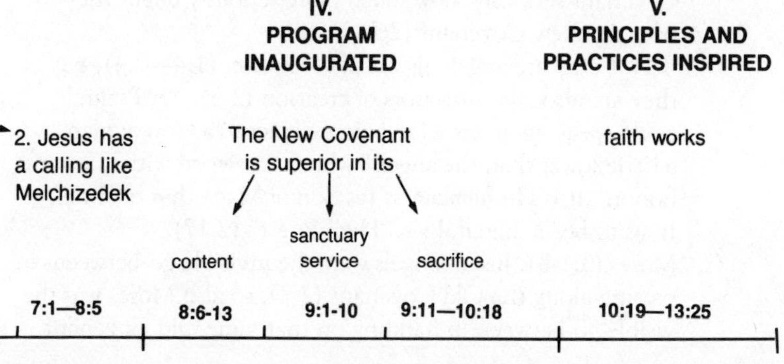

Everything about Hebrews is "better." Christ has a better name than the angels (1:4). He brings in a "better hope" (7:19) because He "has become the guarantee of a better covenant" (7:22). It is a better, or superior covenant because "it is founded on better promises" (8:6). It took "better sacrifices" (9:23) than those old offerings for this better covenant. Because of this betterness we await a "better resurrection" (11:35). The Son's work is superior because His character is superlative.

No wonder we insist that GOD "HAS A BETTER IDEA"! The New Covenant is better than the Old because of

I. *The Person Involved (1:1—3:6)—namely, God's Son, who is superior to:*

A. Prophets (1:1-3)

THE OLD	*THE NEW*
"God spoke" (1:1)	"[God] has spoken" (1:2)
"in the past" (1:1)	"in these last days" (1:2)
"at many times and in various ways" (1:1)	in full and final form

After the author makes seven sterling statements about the Son (in 1:1-3), he goes on to quote seven Scriptures (in 1:4-14).

B. Angels (1:4—2:18). Why angels? Because angels were agents of the old revelation (see Acts 7:53; Gal. 3:19; Heb. 2:2). The Son (agent of the new revelation—1:2, 3) is superior to angels (agents of the old revelation) as is shown by seven Old Testament passages—with five of the seven passages selected from the Psalms. And if the readers treated that Old Covenant seriously, how much more seriously ought they to take the New Covenant (2:2, 3).

Not only are angels agents of revelation (1:4—2:4), but they are also administrators of creation (2:5). Yet Psalm 8 could speak about creation being subject to a "son of man . . . a little lower than the angels" who is "crowned with glory and honor." It is His *humanness* (as Son of Man) that qualifies Jesus to be "a merciful . . . High Priest" (2:17).

C. Moses (3:1-6). Just as angels were the invisible go-betweens in passing along the Old Covenant (2:2), so also Moses was the visible go-between in handing on that same Old Covenant.

As a son over the house, Jesus is superior to Moses the servant. Moses reminds us of that faithless generation under the Old Covenant who failed to enter God's rest. That becomes the jumping-off point for our author's discussion of the current generation who might also fall away from the living God (3:12)

The New Covenant is better than the Old because of:

II. *The Purpose Intended (3:7—4:13)—namely, to provide redemption rest.*

Three themes jet strongly through this section:

A. *Today* (3:7, 13, 15; 4:7) is the day to enter God's rest.

B. There is a "rest" remaining to enter (3:11, 18, 19; 4:1, 3, 5, 6, 9-11).

C. Rest is entered by *faith* (3:12, 18, 19; 4:2, 3, 6). The author's launching pad is Psalm 95:7-11 (quoted in Heb. 3:7-11). The first word in the quotation is "Today," and the last declaration in the quote is "They shall never enter my rest." The author uses that bratty, wilderness generation as a warning flare to his readers. Since he discovers David (probably 400 years after Joshua) still calling for people to enter God's rest "today" (Heb. 4:7, 8), he concludes: "There remains . . . a . . . rest . . . for anyone who enters" (4:9, 10), and "we who have believed enter that rest" (4:3). Believers are rest-enterers. That "word of God" (4:12; from Ps. 95:7-11) judged that generation, and all must give an account. Despite this severe judgment, we have a sympathetic High Priest—and that idea leads to the central thesis (4:14).

The New Covenant is better than the Old because of:

III. *The Priesthood Interposed (4:14—8:5)*

Jesus is a priest? When did He ever wear the colorful priestly uniform? When did He ever officiate in the Jerusalem Temple? This thesis (that Jesus is a priest) was enough to stick in the throat of any Jew. Therefore, the author will have to prove the priesthood of Jesus. But he has a major hurdle—Jesus wasn't even from the correct priestly tribe (7:13, 14). The author overcomes this objection by launching into his sermon text—Psalm 110:4, where God is speaking futuristically about another "priest forever, in the order of Melchizedek." If God had been satisfied with priests from the tribe of Levi, why would he be calling for another, eternal priest compared to Melchizedek (Gen. 14).

Thus, the author states his

A. Thesis: Jesus is a priest with credentials like Aaron (4:14—5:10). Robes and chants don't make priests. Certain credentials do. Priests have to have a:

   1. Human constitution (5:1);
   2. Humane compassion (5:2, 3);
   3. Heavenly calling (5:4).

      Can Jesus match up with these credentials? (Yes. "So Christ also," 5:5.) Consequently, the author uses those three credentials as a checklist, and in reverse fashion (in 5:5-10) buttonhooks Christ into each of these three credentials:

   1. He has a heavenly calling (5:5, 6), as proved by Psalm 2:7 and 110:4;
   2. He has a human constitution (5:7-10);
   3. He has humane compassion (5:7-10). Christ graduated *magna cum laude* from the school of sympathetic suffering!

      That brings the author back to his sermon text (Ps. 110:4 in Heb. 5:10). At this point he bounces off from it as if from a diving board into his pool of thought (5:11—6:20).

B. Parenthesis: Before discussing Melchizedek (his thesis topic) you (says the writer to the readers) need maturity—and you aren't there! At this juncture the author dives into this parenthetical train of thought, only to end up at the point where he dove in. The author then proceeds logically:

   1. Melchizedek, he says: I'd like to talk about him, but you are bottle-babies instead of adults (5:11-14).
   2. Let's leave behind the basics and go on to maturity (6:1-3).
   3. However, maturity is impossible in the case of apostasy. Instead of going on to maturity, apostates have gone back. They've regressed instead of progressed (6:4-8).
   4. But I don't think that's true of you. You must go on to inherit the promises (6:9-12).
   5. Abraham went on to inherit the promises (6:13-15) that God confirmed with an oath (6:16-19).
   6. And (by implication) it was Abraham who met Melchizedek—our postponed topic back at 5:10 (6:20). Therefore, let's go on and talk about Melchizedek (chap. 7).

C. Thesis: Jesus is a priest with a calling like Melchizedek (7:1—8:5). Just about all we can safely say about the king-priest Melchizedek is: he lives. As far as the Genesis record's silence is concerned: "he remains a priest forever" (like the Son of God; 7:3).

If Abraham, who (we might say) was inside Levi, gave to Melchizedek and Melchizedek blessed Abraham, Melchizedek must be greater than Abraham—and, therefore, Melchizedek is greater than Levi (7:4-10).

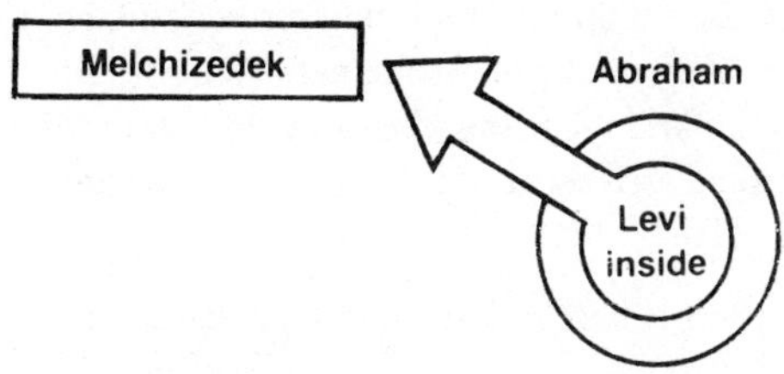

Furthermore, if perfection came via the priesthood of Levi, why would God be predicting a priesthood like Melchizedek (7:11)? Jesus isn't from the Levitical priesthood (7:13, 14), but the superior Melchizedekan priesthood—"on the basis of . . . an indestructible life" (7:16). Still further, God did something with a Melchizedekan priest that He never did with a Levitical priest—went on oath (7:18-22).

We Christians boast an ever-living Priest—and He's just the variety of priest we need (7:23-28). The point in Hebrews is: We do have such a risen, living High Priest in the Person of Jesus who serves in the true, *heavenly* sanctuary (8:1-5).

The New Covenant is better than the Old because of:

IV. *The Program Inaugurated (8:6—10:18)—which requires a better basis, better sanctuary, and better sacrifice.*

A. The Better Covenant (8:6-13). Jeremiah 31:31-34 is the longest Old Testament quote in the New and proposes a "new covenant" (Heb. 8:8). "New" presupposes making the old one "obsolete," just as new computer terminals make old typewriters virtually obsolete.

B. The Better Sanctuary (9:1-10). The separator-curtain in that old "earthly sanctuary" was a parable communicating, "Keep

Out!"—and all the externals didn't meet our conscience's deep need.

C. The Better Sacrifice (9:11—10:18). The superior sacrifice of Christ can cleanse our consciences (9:11-15). Under the Old Covenant virtually everything was ceremcnially cleansed by blood sacrifice (9:16-22). Christ's perfect, perma-sacrifice was a once-for-all sacrifice for sin (9:23-28).

   Furthermore, Christ's sacrifice stands in contrast to those again-and-again, annual, animal sacrifices that can never "take away sins" (10:1-4). Psalm 40:6-8 (quoted in Heb. 10:5-7) shows the inadequacy of those animal sacrifices as over against the voluntary, rational sacrifice of Christ. The annual Old Testament Day of Atonement was actually a way of calling up and recalling one's sins, but when perma-forgiveness arrives, those sacrifices for sins are no longer needed (10:11-18).

The New Covenant is better than the Old because of:

V. *The Principles and Practices Inspired (10:19—13:25)*

A. The Peril of Faithlessness Signaled (10:19-37). The sacrifice of Christ (in 10:1-18), epitomized by "the blood of Jesus" (10:19), "opened for us [the way] . . . to enter the Most Holy Place" (10:19, 20; see also 9:8). This prompts from the author four "let us"es in 10:22-25, including not abandoning the Christian community (10:25) by defecting from the faith.

   This warning flare against apostasy (10:26-31) is referred to as "deliberately keep[ing] on sinning after we have received the knowledge of the truth." Hebrews 10:26-31 should be compared closely with and interpreted together with 6:4-6. (For the argument from the lesser to the greater compare—"if . . . how much more"—2:2, 3; 9:14; 10:26-29; 12:25.)

   Former faithfulness of the readers—epitomized by public persecution, prison ministry, and property confiscation—must not yield to faithlessness (10:32-34).

B. The Principle of Faith Illustrated (10:38—12:4). Faithfulness is the index of faith, for the "righteous one will live by faith" (Hab. 2:4, in Heb. 10:38). This faith text is the springboard to chapter 11—faith's Hall of Fame.

   But what is faith?

"Faith is being sure of what we hope for
and
[faith is being] certain of what we do not see" (11:1).

First, faith is formulated in embodied examples of named Old Testament characters.

1. "By faith Abel . . . was commended as . . . righteous" (11:4), demonstrating the thesis that the "righteous . . . live by faith" (10:38).
2. "By faith Enoch . . . pleased God" (11:5). Therefore, "without faith it is impossible to please God" (11:6), so one must believe that the Unseen One exists.
3. "By faith Noah" dealt with "things not yet seen" (11:7; compare 11:1), becoming "heir of the righteousness that comes by faith" (11:7; 10:38).
4. "By faith Abraham" (11:8) "was looking" (11:10) to a place he'd never seen, and acted accordingly. Abraham faced the future with faith (11:11-19).
5. "By faith Isaac" looked to the "future" (11:20).
6. "By faith Joseph" looked to the future (11:21; compare 11:1a).
7. "By faith Moses" (11:24) . . . "saw him [God] who is invisible" (11:27) because "faith is being . . . certain of what we do not see" (11:1).
8. By faith many mighty miracles occurred (11:28-31).

    Secondly, the author groups a number of miscellaneous and anonymous samples of faith (11:32-40). Four judges, one king, and one prophet-priest exercised faith (11:32). This is followed by the feats (11:33-35a) and "defeats" (11:35b-38) of faith. All are "commended for their faith" (11:39).

    Thirdly, the superlative exemplar of faith and faithfulness (12:1-4) is Jesus. (Ordinarily, we think of Him as the object of our faith, but here He is depicted as the subject of faith to be followed.)

C. The Process of Faith's Discipline (12:5-17). Just as a race (12:1-3) requires discipline, so also a home demands discipline (12:4-11). The readers were under a deluge of difficulties (10:32-34; 12:4). Therefore, the author admonishes them to view their difficulties as divine discipline. Proverbs 3:11, 12 (quoted in Heb. 12:5, 6) urges us to see divine discipline as a sign of spiritual sonship. (To be corrected by God assumes one is a child of God.) This disciplining is not pleasurable, but painful; yet, with a proper response, it can produce the proper results (12:11).

There are two right responses and two wrong responses to divine discipline (12:14-17). Two right responses are for a runner to pursue (1) peace and (2) holiness (12:14). Two wrong responses are (1) bitterness, as if a poisonous plant were rooting within us (12:15), and (2) callousness, as exemplified by Esau who bartered away the precious possession of his birthright.

D. The Peril of Faithlessness Signalled for the Last Time (12:18-29). The Hebrew recipients lived in a world that was shaking—almost like the awe-inspiring scene at Sinai (12:18-21). But they had "not come" to Sinai (12:18); they had "come to Mount Zion, to the heavenly Jerusalem" (12:22). And what a line-up of festive encouragers they could see there by faith (12:22-24)!

   Therefore, in a shaken world, they must listen to "his [God's] voice [who] shook the earth" (12:26) and who promised a heavenquake (!) in Haggai 2:6 (quoted in Heb. 12:26, 27). In the readers' days God was "removing . . . what can be shaken . . . so that what cannot be shaken may remain (12:27), that is, "a kingdom that cannot be shaken" (12:28).

E. The Practices of the Faith-Life (13:1-25). In 20 commands on 15 subjects the author specifies certain practices of the faithful.

   1. Socially (13:1-3), their "brothers" (13:1), "strangers" (13:2), and "prisoners" (13:3) must be treated lovingly.
   2. Domestically, their marriages (13:4) and their money matters (13:5, 6) are to provide contentment rather than covetousness. To reinforce this, Deuteronomy 31:6 and Psalm 118:6, 7 are quoted (in Heb. 13:5, 6).
   3. Theologically, their past leaders are to be remembered (13:7, 8), but "strange teachings" (13:9) are to be refused. Christians don't need to feel second-rate, for "we have an altar" that those former priests can't partake of (13:10), "we . . . have an enduring city" (13:14), and we Christians have our set of sacrifices (13:15, 16). Therefore, their present leaders are to be respected (13:17).
   4. Personally, the author asks prayer for himself (13:18, 19) before praying for his readers (13:20, 21).

In closing, the author mentions tantalizing tidbits about Timothy and Italy (13:22-24). Then he closes with the bedrock of the New Covenant—"grace" (13:25).

No wonder the New Covenant is superior to the Old Covenant! As a little boy once said to Donald Grey Barnhouse—who had just preached an encouraging sermon along these lines, "Boy, doc, we sure are sitting pretty, aren't we?"

NOTES

Chapter 1

[1] A. T. Robertson, *Word Pictures in the New Testament*, V (Nashville: Broadman Press, 1931), p. 328.
[2] E. M. Blaiklock, *Commentary on the New Testament* (Old Tappan, NJ: Revell, 1977), p. 211.
[3] Quoted in Kenneth Wuest's *Untranslatable Riches from the Greek New Testament* (Grand Rapids, MI: Eerdmans's, 1942), p. 13.
[4] A. Skevington Wood, *The Art of Preaching,* (Grand Rapids, MI: Zondervan, 1964), p. 21.
[5] Michael Green, *Christianity Today,* 1 January, 1965.
[6] David McCarthy, *Biblical Expositor and Illuminator,* Winter, 1973-74, p. 26.
[7] *Looking Ahead,* June, 1981.
[8] August van Ryn, *Acts of the Apostles* (New York: Loizeaux Brothers, 1976), p. 70.
[9] Quoted in Ronald Ward's *Royal Sacrament* (London: Marshall, Morgan, and Scott, 1958), p. 32.

Chapter 2

[1] In Carl Henry, ed., *Basic Christian Doctrines* (New York: Holt, Rinehart, and Winston, 1962), p. 67.
[2] William Barclay, *The Letter to the Hebrews* (Philadelphia: Westminster Press, 1947), p. 13.
[3] F. B. Meyer, *The Way into the Holiest* (New York: Revell, 1893), pp. 31, 32.
[4] Philip Hughes, *Commentary on the Epistle to the Hebrews* (Grand Rapids, MI: Eerdmans, 1977), pp. 73, 74.
[5] F. W. Boreham, A *Handful of Stars* (Philadelphia: Judson Press, 1922), p. 195.
[6] Meyer, *The Way,* p. 35.
[7] Merrill Unger, *Stop Existing and Start Living* (Grand Rapids, MI: Eerdmans, 1959), p. 38.

Chapter 3

[1] Vincent Taylor, *The Atonement in the New Testament* (London: Epworth Press, 1945), p. 120.
[2] F. F. Bruce, *Commentary on the Epistle to the Hebrews* (Grand Rapids, MI: Eerdmans, 1964), p. 43.
[3] Byrne J. Horton, *Dictionary of Modern Chess* (Secausus, NJ: Citadel, 1973), p. 187.

Chapter 4

[1] Meyer, *The Way*, pp. 75, 76.
[2] Ibid., p. 68.
[3] Ibid., p. 67.
[4] Augustus Strong, *Systematic Theology* (Westwood, NJ: Revell, 1907), p. 485.

Chapter 5

[1] quoted by Paul Little in *How To Give Away Your Faith* (Downers Grove, IL: Inter-Varsity, 1966), p. 39.
[2] Simon Kistemaker, *Hebrews* (Grand Rapids, MI: Baker, 1984) p. 135.
[3] Hughes, *Hebrews*, p. 169.
[4] See Barclay, *Hebrews*, pp. 39, 40.
[5] From a radio sermon on "The Bible Study Hour," July 28, 1968.

[6] Marcus Dods in *The Expositor's Greek Testament*, IV (Grand Rapids, MI: Eerdmans, 1951), 284.
[7] William Hendriksen, *The Gospel of Luke* (Grand Rapids, MI: Baker, 1976), p. 230.
[8] Alexander Maclaren, *Expositions of Holy Scripture*, XXXII (London: Hodder and Stoughton, 1908), p. 314.
[9] Vernon Grounds, radio sermon on "The Bible Study Hour," July 28, 1968.
[10] Bertrand Russell, *Impact of Science on Society* (Winchester, MA: Allen Unwin, 1976), p. 59
[11] H. R. Mackintosh, *Doctrine of the Person of Jesus Christ* (Edinburgh: T & T Clark, 1912), p. 79.
[12] Hughes, *Hebrews*, p. 186.
[13] Quoted in Grady Davis's *Design for Preaching* (Philadelphia: Fortress, 1958), p. 270.

Chapter 6
[1] Howard Hendricks, *Say It with Love* (Wheaton, IL: Scripture Press, 1975), p. 70.
[2] *The Chicago Tribune*, June 13, 1981.
[3] W. E. Vine, *The Epistle to the Hebrews* (London: Oliphants, 1952).
[4] Grant Osborne in *Grace Unlimited* (Minneapolis, MN: Bethany House, 1975).
[5] Meyer, *The Way*, p. 120
[6] *Decision* magazine.
[7] Spicq, *Commentary on the Epistle to the Hebrews.*
[8] Barclay, *The Letter to the Hebrews*, p. 64.
[9] Berkeley Mickelsen, *The Biblical Expositor*, III (Philadelphia: A. J. Holman, 1960), p. 396.

Chapter 7
[1] Robert Louis Stevensen, "The Sire de Maletroit's Door," *A Book of Short Stories* (New York: D. Appleton and Co., 1920), p. 35.
[2] In F. E. Marsh, *The Greatest Book in Literature* (London: Hulbert, 1929), p. 89.
[3] Davis, *Design for Preaching*, p. 207.
[4] Quoted in Ralph Martin, *New Testament Foundations*, II (Grand Rapids, MI: Eerdmans, 1978), 349.
[5] *Antiquities, 20.227.*
[6] J. Wilbur Chapman, *Our Daily Bread.*
[7] H. A. Guy, *The New Testament Doctrine of the 'Last Things,'* (London: Oxford University, 1948), p. 132.
[8] Barclay, *Hebrews*, p. xv.

Chapter 8
[1] *William Barclay: A Spiritual Biography* (Grand Rapids, MI: Eerdmans, 1975), p. 14.
[2] Hughes, *Hebrews*, p. 311.
[3] Steven Barabas, *Zondervan Pictorial Bible Dictionary* (Grand Rapids, MI: Zondervan, 1963), pp. 180, 181.
[4] Leon Morris, *The Apostolic Preaching of the Cross* (Grand Rapids, MI: Eerdmans, 1955), p. 86.
[5] Barclay, *A New Testament Wordbook* (New York: Harper and Brothers), p. 31.
[6] A. P. Gibbs, *A Preacher and His Preaching* (New York: Loizeaux Brothers, 1958), pp. 179, 180.
[7] Oscar Cullman in Michael Green's *Evangelism in the Early Church* (Grand Rapids, MI: Eerdmans, 1970), p. 140.

Chapter 9
[1] Donald Miller, *Fire in Thy Mouth* (New York: Abingdon, 1954), p. 82.
[2] Ward, *Royal Sacrament*, p. 68.
[3] Benjamin Warfield, *The Person and Work of Christ* (Philadelphia: Presbyterian and Reformed, 1950), p. 425.

[4] Quoted in Hughes, p. 426.
[5] Alva McClain, *Romans: The Gospel of God's Grace* (Chicago: Moody Press, 1973), p. 16.

Chapter 10

[1] Kistemaker, *Hebrews, p. 319*
[2] Hagner, *Hebrews*, p. 166.
[3] Donald G. Barnhouse, *God's Heirs* (Wheaton, IL: Van Kampen Press, 1953), p. 169.
[4] John Henry Jowett, *God Our Contemporary* (New York: Revell, 1922), p. 46.
[5] Radio sermon, February 11, 1984.
[6] Kistemaker, *Hebrews*, p. 322.
[7] F. E. Marsh, *Emblems of the Holy Spirit* (Grand Rapids, MI: Kregel, 1959), p. 206
[8] According to Liz Harris, *The New Yorker*, September 16, 1985; p. 62.
[9] Diane Ketcham, *Tempo* section of *The Chicago Tribune*, October 17, 1985.
[10] Norman Grubb, *C. T. Studd* (Chicago: Moody Press, 1933), pp. 89, 90.

Chapter 11

[1] Meyer, *The Way*, p. 205.
[2] Ibid., p. 206.
[3] Robertson, *Word Pictures*, V, p.433.
[4] Edward Carnell, *The Kingdom of Love and the Pride of Life* (Grand Rapids, MI: Eerdmans, 1960), p. 135.
[5] Quoted in Charles Bradshaw's *You and Your Teen* (Elgin, IL: David C. Cook Publishing Co., 1985).
[6] Jay Adams, *Competent to Counsel* (Philadelphia: Presbyterian and Reformed, 1970), p. 166.
[7] Robertson, *Word Pictures*, V, p. 437.
[8] Quoted in Erik Routley, *Hymns and the Faith* (Grand Rapids, MI: Eerdmans, 1968), p. 27.
[9] November 3, 1967
[10] Quoted in F. W. Boreham, *A Faggot of Torches* (Philadelphia: Judson, 1926), p. 261.
[11] Ibid., pp. 262, 263.
[12] Meyer, *The Way*, p. 231.
[13] Ibid., p. 235.

Chapter 12

[1] Kistemaker, *Hebrews*, p. 409.
[2] Dibelius and Conzelmann, *The Pastoral Epistles* (Philadelphia: Fortress, 1972), p. 49.
[3] According to Richard Niebuhr, *Christ and Culture* (New York: Harper, 1951), p. 168.
[4] De la Cruz and La Veck, *Human Sexuality and The Mentally Retarded* (Baltimore: Penguin, 1974), p. 61.
[5] Richard Ult, *Good News* magazine.
[6] Thomas Miller, *Christianity Today*, 21 October 1983.
[7] Richard Ult, *Good News Magazine*.
[8] Martin Marty, *Christianity Today*, 21 October 1983.
[9] Cornelius Plantinga, Jr., *Beyond Doubt* (Grand Rapids, MI: Bible Way, 1980), p. 84.
[10] Hughes, *Hebrews*, p. 574.
[11] Kistemaker, *Hebrews*, p. 427.
[12] George Turner, *The New and Living Way*, (Minneapolis, MN: Bethany Fellowship, 1975), p. 188.

Directions for Group Leaders

The questions and projects below should form the framework of the actual time spent in group discussion. The week before every class the leader ought to assign both the lesson and the Bible passage (found under each chapter title) to be read for the upcoming class so that students will come to class with an informational foundation for the discussion.

Some class members may come without having read the lesson for the week. It would be wise to have a plan for including them in a short review session before jumping into the study proper. Perhaps two or three other class members could give an "overview report" with highlights from the reading. Certain portions of the book could be read aloud. Or, you could set up a short dialogue session between two who have read the lesson content. However you do it, make sure the unprepared members feel every bit as important to the class as the others.

The New International Version, 1984 edition, is the Bible translation quoted throughout the commentary, although the study can be conducted using any helpful translation. Remember to read the directions for each chapter at least a week before class. That way, you will have adequate time to pull together some of the special learning experiences requiring advance preparation.

To encourage group discussion, don't be shy about asking, "Susan, in what ways has this issue been a part of your own life experience?" If someone responds to a question, you can add something like, "How have others of you dealt with this?"

Don't be afraid of respectful disagreement, for we can learn from people who differ from us. Even if you don't agree, you can comment, "I don't think I agree, but it will certainly give us something to think about. How do others of you feel?" The secret of effective group discussion is to keep throwing open-ended questions (*not* questions that can be answered with a mere "yes" or "no") back to members of the group. Be sure to acknowledge people's contributions: "Thanks for sharing that, David. I know it took some courage to bring that up."

Try to include in all your group sessions some of the key ingredients for building group life: a time for sharing, a time for prayer, and perhaps light refreshments around which significant conversation can take place. Bible study groups can be much more that just an intellectual trip. They can become a means of developing strong bonds of Christian fellowship.

Below, three items will be found for each of the 12 class sessions:

A. A Need-hook. Each week this paragraph will provide a discussion item with which to open class. Normally it will try to hook into some felt need humans experience that will in turn tie into a major truth emerging from the Bible passage to be studied. Hence, the leader moves the class from a felt need to the Bible principles.

B. Fun Feature(s). Every week the leader is provided with an activity (to do or discuss) with an element of group action or even humor involved. This group game or project will sensitize the students to an idea or issue from the particular passage being studied.

C. For Group Discussion. While there are usually a number of questions included within the body of the commentary at pertinent points in the flow of the study, seven to ten extra application questions on each given Bible passage are supplied here. The leader should allow plenty of time for students to think about and respond to the questions. If all questions and activities are used, the class time will probably take about an hour (although by selectivity in the use of the questions, the class time could be made shorter).

Happy study and good grouping to you!

CHAPTER 1

A. A Need-hook

1. In groups of two or three, discuss what planet Earth would be like if God had made no communication with it. With whom have you enjoyed close communication (preferably other than a spouse)? What value accrued from that close communication?

2. Share a time when you felt your world (like that of the Hebrews) seemed to be tumbling in.

B. Fun Features

1. Brainstorm as many ways as you can that humans communicate. Do the same with ways God has communicated.

2. From a pile of magazines and newspapers let small groups cut out all the means of communicating that they can spot. Share these with the whole group after five minutes of hunting.

C. For Group Discussion

1. Hebrews 1:1 implies a great variety in God communication through the ages. What is one unusual form of communication you've witnessed that has stuck in your mind?

2. Can you recall some occasion when a letter (like Hebrews) carried spiritual content that helped you?

3. What current ideas, people, and isms is God's Son superior to, and in what ways?

4. What are some experiences you recall when you felt that God got through to you?

5. Hebrews 1:1-4 is a highly poetic presentation of the person of Christ. Can you think of some elevated hymn or hymn line about Christ? What do you think poetry contributes to our understanding of God or Christ?

6. Can you think of a verse from "his powerful word" (1:3) that has impacted you on some occasion?

7. A catharsis is an emotional cleansing. Christ's death (1:3) is a kind of catharsis. Can you recall an experience when you felt that you had just stepped out of the shower, spiritually speaking?

8. The Son is heir of all and is "at the right hand of the Majesty in heaven" (1:3). What psychological tone-up could this sense of awesome majesty contribute to an office clerk, farm worker, or housewife's day?

CHAPTER 2

A. A Need-hook

1. See how many actual contexts (e.g., epithets pasted on history's rulers' names, such as "Catherine the Great"; commercials like Tony the Tiger's advertising cereal as "gr-r-reat"; etc.) your small groups can think of that use the term "great." What's so "great" (2:3) about salvation?

2. In an assigned amount of time, ask your small groups to quote the substance of as many Bible verses as they can (just as the author of Hebrews cites seven verses in 1:5-14). Ask: How much of the Bible do you think we could reconstruct if an enemy conquered our country and we were placed in concentration camps without Bibles?

B. Fun Feature

Let your small groups momentarily take over their country's postal system (in their imaginations). Bring along some appropriately funny prize to award to the group that comes up with the most creative alternative idea for the standard way now used to convey messages. (Then tie this in with the two sets of messengers in Hebrews 1 and 2—angels and the Son.)

C. For Group Discussion

1. What practical values can you think of for angels?
2. Jehovah's Witnesses believe that Jesus was the same as Michael the archangel in a preexistent state. What would the author of Hebrews think of this view? Support your answer from Hebrews 1.
3. Hebrews 1:5 stresses a close Father-Son relationship. What do you appreciate about your relationship with your human father? If you did not have a close relationship with your earthly father, what would you have wanted most, and how might God help to fill in that gap?
4. The angels worship Christ (1:6). What does worship mean to you? How might it become more meaningful?
5. Hebrews 1:7 compares God's messengers to "winds" and "flames." What items can you come up with to compare them to?
6. If Christ "hated wickedness" (1:9), what forms of wickedness do you think present-day Christians ought to be hating, and why? In what specific ways can we combat those wickednesses?
7. Name one thing that has brought you joy (1:9).
8. Angels are serving Christians (1:14). Name two specific ways you are familiar with that one Christian is serving someone else. In what ways would you like to be served?

CHAPTER 3

A. A Need-hook

1. Let groups of three come up with a composite list of qualities to form a "Mr. Meanie" version of a job supervisor. After sharing lists, make the transition to the kind of an international supervisor that the new world will someday be subjected to (2:5ff).
2. See if small groups can compile a list of the kinds of barriers existing in cross-cultural communication (e.g., learning slang expressions, such as "we're in the same boat" or "he threw me a curve"). Point: Sharing sameness has its value. Move then to the assets accruing from the fact that Jesus shares our humanity (2:14).

B. Fun Feature

While someone in each group draws his or her cartoon-style picture of an extraterrestrial alien, let the small groups talk about funny equipment features that this alien will need to cope with some of humanity's needs and eccentric behaviors.

C. For Group Discussion

1. What implications would you draw for your life from the fact that God has a mind full of ("mindful of," 2:6) humanity?

2. If God intended to "put everything under" (2:8) humanity's care, what application does this have for earth's ecology? What is one area of ecological concern facing your community? What can members of the class do to confront that issue?

3. In Hebrews 2:8, 9 we sense the incongruity between the way things ought to be on our planet and the way things are. What examples from your experience can you cite to illustrate the incongruity between the way things are and the way things ought to be in our world?

4. How can we help people "get on the train" "in bringing many sons [and daughters] to glory" (2:10)?

5. How do you think you will face death when it comes? What stories about the dying can you share (2:14, 15)?

6. What actual case can you recall of someone—like Jesus—being "merciful" (2:17)?

7. What helps you to "fix your thoughts on Jesus" (3:1)?

8. Moses and Christ were faithful (3:5, 6). What are two areas of faithfulness you can approve yourself for? What are two areas of faithfulness you would like to improve?

CHAPTER 4

A. A Need-hook

1. What song titles, book characters, TV actors or characters can your small groups use to illustrate human restlessness? After combining the results of your findings, comment upon the solution to this emphasis from 4:1, 9, and 11.

2. Let parents share stories of brattiness, either from their own children's stubbornness or their childhood memories. From these illustrations turn to the frequent brattiness (3:8-10) of the Israelites in disobeying God.

B. Fun Feature

Provide pieces of paper for each individual with a simple drawing of an island of the paper. Read aloud the instructions for the "Life Game" from page 39. Give student's about ten minutes to draw their own life maps. Following that, let them share this spiritual map with one other person in the group. If you wish, each person could share one meaningful item he or she has learned about his or her partner with the whole group.

C. For Group Discussion

1. Can you think of a time when you hardened yourself (3:7) in some area? Do you know of any cases when God softened the heart of someone who was hard?
2. Is there a time in your life that you would describe as a "desert" time (3:8)? Would you share something of what it involved?
3. Who or what has encouraged (3:13) you lately? What are two ways that you'd like to be encouraged?
4. In what area of Christian experience do you have the most difficulty believing (3:15; 4:6)?
5. The expression "mixed with faith" (4:2, KJV) makes us think of the field of chemistry. Are there other high school or college subjects you took that might make helpful illustrations of some Christian experience?
6. Can you think of one specific way that the Word of God has been "living and active" (4:12) in you or someone you know during this past month?
7. Daniel Webster said that his profoundest thought was that there was a God "to whom we must give account" (4:13). What is one area in which you would like to pray with another Christian about becoming more accountable to God?

CHAPTER 5

A. A Need-hook

If you were a girl who had just discovered that she was pregnant out of wedlock, what kind of a person would you want to go talk to first? Let pairs discuss this and have one person report one major point. Make the transition to the idea of sinners going to Jesus our sympathetic Priest.

B. Fun Feature

Give groups of four several minutes to act out a humorous scene where someone is having a difficult time *getting through to* someone else (e.g., waiting in a grocery line; calling a department store to report a complaint on a newly installed washer; etc.). After the dramatic troupes have had fun presenting their short skits, talk about the idea of an *approachable* God—where we don't have to cut through the red tape of bureaucracy in order to approach God acceptably. We have an Introducer in Jesus.

C. For Group Discussion

1. Do you think there's a difference between sympathizing with someone's weakness (4:15) and falling prey to someone's whining and self-pity? If so, how would you distinguish the two?
2. Describe one person you think of as approachable (4:16). If someone feels he is not particularly approachable, how can you help him in that area?
3. Can you recall some "time of need" (4:16) when God tailored His answer to that occasion?
4. What kind of a Christian do you think would be least likely to "deal gently" (5:2) with, say, a recently converted gambler or prostitute? What helps a person learn to "deal gently" with other sinners?
5. Jesus had a strong sense of His calling in what He did (5:5, 6). Do you think we need a calling for our vocation? Do you think Christians need a strong sense of security about themselves, their gifts, etc.? If so, how can that be heightened?
6. Do you think Jesus got a positive answer to His prayer in Gethsemane (5:7)? If so, what form might that answer have taken? When do you think strong emotions (5:7) are appropriate?
7. Would you share one lesson you feel that you have learned through some particular suffering (5:8)?

CHAPTER 6

A. A Need-hook

Billy Graham had a close friend and co-worker in the early days of Youth for Christ. After attending a seminary that intensified this friend's doubts about the Bible's trustworthiness, he left the ministry and the faith. Do you think such a person was a Christian? How do you account for this loss of faith? Have you known of any similar people? (Move from this to a discussion of Heb. 6:4-6.)

B. Fun Features

1. Use someone's set of encyclopedias. Divide into small teams. Give the teams five minutes to list as many individuals and items as they can from the encyclopedia that relate in some way to the idea of perseverance (or keeping on).
2. Ahead of time phone class members and have each participant bring one photo of himself or herself when he or she was a baby or any age up to twenty years old. Mix the photos up and let each person guess who belongs to each picture. Come up with a crazy prize for the

person who gets the most right. Then move to the concept of spiritual age level in 5:11-14.

C. For Group Discussion

1. Do you think all Christians are supposed to be teachers? If not, how would you explain 5:12?
2. What two helps or skills would you recommend for Christians who want to train "themselves to distinguish good from evil" (5:14)? What life situation can you recall when you learned a lesson about distinguishing good from evil?
3. From the Greek word behind "trained" (5:14) we get our English word gymnasium. How many parallels can you see between gymnastics and moral choices?
4. What does "repentance" (6:1, 6) mean to you?
5. How do you feel when someone is "confident" (6:9) about you and what you will do? How does this compare with other kinds of motivation (e.g., fear)? Can you give an illustration of such confidence as manifested in your parent-and-child experience?
6. Can you think of a time when diligence and perseverance (6:11) paid off for you?
7. What is one Biblical promise (6:13-15) that has meant a lot to you? Explain why.
8. Can you think of a living illustration of hope and of hopelessness (6:18, 19)?

CHAPTER 7

A. A Need-hook

Lead students in naming and discussing various ways people try to prolong this life and come to terms with death (e.g., face-lifts disguise aging). Move from this discussion to how that felt need is satisfied ultimately in the Ever-living One (7:16, 25).

B. Fun Features

1. Have each student write his or her own humorous epitaph (e.g., "He was the guy whose ties were always out of style."). Move to the fact that most of us prefer to dodge thinking about death, yet as Shakespeare said, we also have "immortal longings" within us. Turn to 7:16 and 25.
2. Let small groups have a five-minute contest to compile a list of almost unpronouncable names (like Mr. Snuffleupagus on Sesame Street). From there shift to the Hebrews 7 treatment of Melchizedek—not your everyday byword.

C. For Group Discussion

1. Melchizedek was a bonified priest outside of the Hebrew tradition. Can you think of people or ideas outside of your particular stream of Christian tradition that have broadened your perspective?

2. As Hebrews' author assessed it, Melchizedek (the almost unheard-of) was greater than Abraham (7:4). Can you tell about someone whose spiritual stature has grown in your thinking over the course of time?

3. What would you say that the argument of Hebrews 7 is in not more than five sentences?

4. Hebrews 7:12 speaks of a major change being instituted. How do you respond to change? Why do you think it is so difficult sometimes for Christians (who believe they are converted or changed people) to change? What has been one traumatic change for you?

5. Hebrews 7:18 speaks about an institution "set aside because it was . . . useless." What is one tradition that you think may have outlived its usefulness? How can you determine when a long-standing tradition needs changing?

6. We live under "a better covenant" (7:22). What do you think a greater sense of covenant awareness might contribute to God's people in your locale?

7. Hebrews 7:25 says Christ "is able to save completely those who come to God through him." Would you share one story about someone in whom you have witnessed this truth happening?

CHAPTER 8

A. A Need-hook

Have you ever got caught by the fine print of some policy? What is one benefit you value in a particular insurance policy? Have you ever gotten taken in by the guarantee of some person or company?

These questions will enable you to move into the benefits of God's Insurance Policy in Hebrews 8:6-13.

B. Fun Features

1. Pass out paper and pencils to your small groups. Let them confer and come up with their own zany insurance policy and company name. Have one representative from each group share the benefits and catches with all the groups. Move them to Hebrews 8:6-13.

2. Pass out paper and pencils to your small groups. Let them compile a list of as many treaties, covenants, agreements as they can (from early childhood tree-house club agreements to international accords).

Let each group share their findings. Then move to the covenant idea in 9:15-17.

C. For Group Discussion

1. Have you ever served as a mediator in any situation? What did you do that might throw light on what Jesus has done as our Mediator (8:6)?
2. Can you give a living illustration of the difference of some truth having been internalized (8:10) as over against a merely external truth?
3. What do you think Hebrews 8:11 might have to say to a pastor who prohibited a group from having a home Bible study because he couldn't be there?
4. What words or illustrations would you use to describe a cleared conscience (9:9, 14)? If someone asked you to define "conscience" what would you say?
5. Can you give a modern illustration of the danger of Christians getting reentrapped in "external regulations" (9:10) while missing spiritual essentials?
6. How would you reply to someone who stated that the God of the Old Testament was a fiendish blood lover?
7. Christ appeared "to do away with sin" (9:26). How would you reply to someone who rejoined, "But if you still sin, then He hasn't done away with sin, has He?"
8. How would you depict someone who is "waiting for him" (9:28)?

CHAPTER 9

A. A Need-hook

Divide students into small groups and let them compile a list of symbolic actions and body language people use. For instance, rolling up the sleeves can symbolize, "I'm ready to get to work." Or, owning a large library would symbolize that so-and-so is a college professor. A tight, short-sleeved T-shirt might epitomize Mr. Macho, etc.

After groups share their lists, move into the introductory paragraphs of this chapter in the study book—sharing how the unceasing motion of Old Testament priests signified that (unlike Christ) their sacrificial work was never completed.

B. Fun Feature

Let small groups come up with some of their pet peeves of words or phrases they may hear repeated ("*You know* how people repeat things, *you know*?"). After sharing examples, turn to (1) the repetitious actions of Old Testament priests, and (2) the repetition of "let us" in 10:22-25.

C. For Group Discussion

1. How might Hebrews 10 help believers who are feeling "guilty for their sins" (10:2)? What truths are essential to understand in order to prevent this problem?
2. What different tacks have humans taken throughout history to deal with their sins (10:14)?
3. As with the psalmist in Hebrews 10:5, have you ever had to revise your understanding about what pleases God? If so, how?
4. What kind of mental picture do you have of being holy (10:10, 14)? What are some distorted views people have about being holy?
5. Do you think having "confidence" (10:19) in a Godward relationship and "draw[ing] near to God . . . in full assurance" (10:22) affect one's psychological and social well-being or not? Explain and support your answer.
6. What are some spin-off values of the habit of "meeting together" (10:25) as Christians?
7. Have you ever known anyone who ever threw overboard his or her Christian faith (10:26-31)? Share what happened. Did you see any telltale signs that it would happen? What are ways it can be prevented?
8. Have you ever felt that you had to stand "your ground" (10:32) as a believer? Share the circumstances.
9. Have you ever had any experience with visiting those in prison or who have suffered losses (10:34)? If so, share the particulars of those experiences.

CHAPTER 10

A. A Need-hook

Make up a series of slips of paper for each student in class. On each slip write something like:

(1) "By faith when her house burned down, she . . ."

(2) "By faith when he got a great job promotion, he . . ."

(3) "By faith she navigated her way through widowhood by . . ."

Pass out these slips with a pencil to each student. Let them fill in the remainder of the sentence on each slip. Then ask each person to read how he or she has filled in the blank.

B. Fun Feature

In groups of four have students write a modern version of Hebrews

11, filling in the faith feats and "defeats" with specific names of people they know. For example,

"By faith Myrtle Traborne visited her elderly neighbor on a regular basis."

"By faith Harry Osgood decided not to accept a job transfer, since it would mean less time with his family," etc.

Let the groups share aloud their completed compositions.

C. For Group Discussion

1. Do you see a distinction between initial saving faith and the faith of Hebrews 11? If so, how would you express that distinction?
2. What is one truth you "understand" by faith (11:3) that you might not otherwise?
3. Would you share how the life of someone who has died still speaks (11:4) to you?
4. Can you name one way your "earnestly seek"ing has been rewarded (11:6)?
5. Give an illustration of how fear (11:7) can be compatible with faith.
6. Would you share a case of the seeming absurdity (from the world's viewpoint; 11:13) of acting in faith?
7. Do you think many middle-class Americans lose the pilgrim sense (11:13) of faith? If so, how might it be restored?
8. Have you ever felt that you had to sacrifice something of considerable value for God (11:17)?
9. What is one future aspect (11:20-22) of your faith?
10. Can you think of cases where virtually the opposite things (see 11:32-38) were accomplished by faith?

CHAPTER 11

A. A Need-hook

Let class members recall one instance of undergoing discipline (e.g., saving money for a special present, etc.). After sharing, move the class into the discipline of the racetrack and home front in 12:1-13.

B. Fun Features

1. Have class members clip out of old newspapers one illustration of discipline gleaned from an article or picture of some sporting event. Let them share the gist of their findings. What have they learned from sports? Then turn to the sports illustration of 12:1-3.
2. Let class members share a recollection of some childhood

warning—that may not necessarily have been heeded—and the results. Make the transition to the last warning passage in Hebrews (12:14-29).

C. For Group Discussion

1. Can you recall a time when you became aware that someone was witnessing (12:1) your actions—for better or for worse?
2. Would you share an example of "struggle against sin" (12:4) you have read or known about?
3. Can you remember an example of parental discipline (12:7-9)—amusing or otherwise?
4. What are some ways believers may need to "make every effort to live in peace" (12:14)? What are some examples of trying to preserve a false peace?
5. Can you recall a time when you threw away an opportunity (12:16, 17) that you later regretted?
6. If there are any mountain climbers in the group, they may want to share some mountain-related experience (12:18-21) that has taught them something about God.
7. Do you think non-Christians today relate positively to the element of warning (12:25)?
8. Have you undergone a time of memorable shake-up (12:26-28) in your life? What insights did you gather from it?
9. What does "reverence" (12:28) mean to you? For example, some say: reverence means being quiet prior to the beginning of a church service. If so, does that mean talking with people afterward is irreverent?

CHAPTER 12

A. A Need-hook

Encourage each participant to recall a time when he or she felt the need for the interest of another human (e.g., being thrown into a new elementary school class after moving to a new location; visiting a church for the first time; etc.). From the shared experiences make the transition to the author's encouragement to do this very thing for strangers and prisoners (12:3, 3). After that, let the class brainstorm particular groups and individuals whom they might be reaching out to touch.

B. Fun Feature

Since this session will be partly a review of Hebrews, give small groups about seven minutes alone in order to come up with a pantomime skit (i.e., no talking allowed) to present in groups to the rest of the class. Each skit should reflect some truth, teaching, memorable verse, or illustration from their study of Hebrews. (They may resort to their Bibles if needed.)

C. For Group Discussion

1. Have you ever been blessed by being hospitable to someone (13:2)? Would you share it with the group?
2. What erroneous or unbiblical notions have you heard on the subject of sex (13:4)?
3. Have you ever felt convicted about possession of things (13:5)? Have you found any inventory questions helpful to guard against things-ism?
4. Do you have in your memory bank a recollection of how some Christian leader exhibited personal care for you (13:7, 17)?
5. Can you illustrate some "strange teachings" (13:9) you have encountered?
6. Is there a painful experience of mistreatment (13:3) or "disgrace" (13:13) you might tell about?
7. Can you recall any leadership capacity when your "work" was "a joy not a burden" (13:17)?
8. Has there been a time when someone exhorted you (13:22) in such a way that proved beneficial?
9. Let the class members share favorite memories from their study of the Book of Hebrews. Since the author urges "pray for us" (13:18), divide up the group into threes and close by praying for each other.

Dr. Jim Townsend is Bible Editor for the David C. Cook Publishing Co. A former pastor and instructor at Mid-South Bible College (Memphis, TN), he is a graduate of Emmaus Bible School, Bryan College, Dallas Theological Seminary, and Fuller Theological Seminary.